# Crime and the
# Responsible
# Community

# Crime and the Responsible Community

The 1979 LONDON LECTURES
IN CONTEMPORARY CHRISTIANITY

EDITORS:
John Stott *and* Nick Miller

*WILLIAM B. EERDMANS PUBLISHING COMPANY*
*Grand Rapids*

Copyright © 1980 by the Management Committee of the London Lectures in Contemporary Christianity.
First published 1980 by Hodder and Stoughton Ltd., England.
This American edition published 1980 through special arrangement with Hodder and Stoughton by Wm. B. Eerdmans Publishing Co., 255 Jefferson Ave. S.E. Grand Rapids, MI 49503
All rights reserved
Printed in the United States of America

# Contents

# Foreword

by John Stott, Chairman of the London Lectures' Committee

The title of the 1979 London Lectures in Contemporary Christianity, *Crime and the Responsible Community*, contains a deliberate *double entendre*. It acknowledges on the one hand that society, by the conditions of poverty, bad housing, unemployment etc. which it permits, has a share in the breeding of criminals, and on the other that every civilized society will develop responsibly constructive attitudes towards them. The implications of this double responsibility were examined in the summer of 1979 by a team of five Christian lecturers, one American and four British. In the light of divine revelation and of human research, they probed the origins of crime and the treatment of criminals, the facts and fancies surrounding police and prisons, how to prevent delinquency and how to rehabilitate the delinquent.

The purpose of the annual London Lectures is to contribute a Christian perspective to some topic of current debate. Both in hearing the lectures and in reading the book, I have been impressed by two characteristics of this year's contribution.

First, the contributors together possess a remarkable breadth of expertise. Chuck Colson has been consecutively a successful lawyer, a prison inmate and the founder of the Prison Fellowship. Norman Anderson has been a distinguished academic specializing in Islamic law, was until recently Director of London University's Institute of Advanced Legal Studies, and has a lucid legal mind. David McNee as London's Police Commissioner occupies a hot seat, whose temperature is uncomfortably high at the moment; he is well aware of public criticism of the police and is anxious to improve relations with the whole community, especially the ethnic minorities. Bob Holman renounced a university chair in social administration in order to pioneer an impressive community project on a housing estate. And Mike Jenkins, having given twenty years to the prison service as borstal housemaster, staff tutor and prison governor, is still asking searching questions about the very establishment to which by profession he belongs. Here then is a group of theoreticians and practitioners (some of whom are both), who give us an unusual combination of scholarly critique and constructive proposal. They know the problems at first hand. So they refuse either to duck them or to offer superficial solutions.

Secondly, all the contributors to this book are united in their Christian convictions. Throughout the discussion their faith in God as both creator and redeemer colours their attitude to human beings and social structures. They are determined to preserve the unique worth of men and women made in God's image, to maintain their human dignity by holding them responsible for their actions, and to oppose everything in society (including the evils of imprisonment) which dehumanizes them. Our contributors look beyond the fact of creation, however, to the possibility of redemption. From Scripture, history and experience, they know the power of the gospel to redeem, renew and transform even the most unpromising people, and to make them like Christ. It is this confidence in the gospel which makes them anxious to see Christians taking fresh initiatives in the fields of prevention and rehabilitation, in befriending prisoners and in helping them when discharged to return to normal life. The lectures were attended by many hundreds of alert and appreciative listeners. Now that they have been published, they should command an even wider audience. This is the first time the London Lectures have been delivered by a team rather than by a single lecturer. The book is therefore a symposium, and readers will detect some unevenness of treatment, a little overlap and even a few differences of opinion. These creases have not been artificially ironed out. The chapters follow the same sequence as the lectures, except that Charles Colson's second contribution has appropriately become the last chapter of the book. Notes and bibliographical references have been relegated to the end of each chapter.

I express my warm gratitude to Nick Miller for his advice in the early planning of these lectures, his editorial labours in the production of this book and his perceptive postscript; to the members of the 'Crime, Law and Punishment' group of the Shaftesbury Project, chaired by Nick Miller, who made helpful suggestions on the first drafts of the lectures; and to

Tom Cooper, my study assistant, who showed considerable enthusiasm both in shouldering the organization of the lectures and in assisting Nick Miller in the editing of this book.

September 1979

# Some Biographical Details of the Contributors

*Charles Colson.* Mr Colson is Founder and Director of the Prison Fellowship, Washington D.C. He had a distinguished career as a young lawyer and in political circles in Washington before becoming Special Counsel to President Nixon in 1969. He served seven months in prison for his part in the Watergate affair. He has written two books *Born Again* (1976) and *Life Sentence* (1979).

*Sir Norman Anderson*, OBE, QC, FBA, was formerly Director of the Institute of Advanced Legal Studies and Professor of Oriental Laws in the University of London. He has been Chairman of the House of Laity in the Church of England's General Synod and is the author of several books, on both legal and Christian themes, including *Issues of Life and Death*, the 1975 London Lectures.

*Sir David McNee*, QPM, has been Commissioner of the Metropolitan Police since 1977. He joined the Glasgow City police as a constable in 1946 and had an outstanding career in Scotland which led to his appointment as Chief Constable of Glasgow in 1971. Then in 1975, when the Glasgow City force was merged with five others to form the Strathclyde Police, he was appointed the first Chief Constable of Strathclyde.

*Dr Bob Holman* first worked as a Local Authority Child Care Officer. He then held academic appointments in the Universities of Glasgow and Birmingham before being appointed Professor of Social Administration at the University of Bath. In 1976 he took up a post with the Church of England Children's Society as a Community Social Worker on a council housing estate. He has written several books, including *Poverty: Explanations of Social Deprivation* (1978), and contributes regularly to social work and other journals.

*Michael Jenkins* graduated in law and applied social studies and has worked for twenty years in the Prison Service, as borstal housemaster, staff tutor and, until 1977, Governor of Oxford Prison. He is now working on the operational side of the Prison Department in Birmingham.

*Nick Miller* works for a London Borough's Social Services Department as a research officer. He graduated in law and social administration and spent four years working at the Institute of Criminology in the University of Cambridge. He convenes the 'Crime, Law and Punishment' group of the Shaftesbury Project.

# I  Towards an Understanding of the Origins of Crime

Charles Colson

**Introduction**
The London Lectures Committee has given me the task of describing the origins of crime and society's response to it. I think it is only fair to tell you at the outset that a team of researchers in America, composed of an eminent psychiatrist, Dr Samuel Yochelson (now deceased) and an eminent psychologist, Dr Stanton Samenow, completed two years ago a sixteen-year study of the origins of crime.[1] After those many years of research, which included hundreds of lengthy interviews with over two hundred and fifty individuals, they came to the conclusion that it is impossible to identify any single cause of crime. Nonetheless, with what you Britons would regard as typical American bravado, I will plunge in and attempt to do in two hours what Yochelson and Samenow could not do in sixteen years. I suspect that I was chosen for this task because of my personal familiarity with the origins of crime, situated as I was in the centre of one of the great political scandals of modern times. Perhaps that is qualification enough.

There are few topics other than crime which are of greater public concern on either side of the Atlantic. In America, for example, according to the Federal Bureau of Investigation's *Uniform Crime Reports*, the chances of being murdered, robbed, raped or victimized by aggravated assault *tripled* in the sixteen years between 1960 and 1976.

Charles Silberman, in his excellent book *Criminal Violence, Criminal Justice* observes that 'if recent rates continue, at least three Americans in every hundred will be the victims of a violent crime this year, and one household in ten will be burglarized.'[2]

These are frightening, even terrifying, statistics, and although America has the highest crime rate of any of the seventy-nine industrialized nations of the Western world, the

problem of crime is, of course, universal. It has always been
with us and it always will be with us. For, as the former
director of Cambridge University's Institute of Criminology
Sir Leon Radzinowicz has written, 'No national characteristic, no political régime, no system of law, police, justice,
punishment, treatment or even terror has rendered a country
exempt from crime.'[3]

*The definition of crime*

Most people would agree with Edwin Sutherland's definition:
'The essential characteristic of crime is that it is behaviour
which is prohibited by the State as an injury to the State and
against which the State may react, at least as a last resort, by
punishment. The two abstract criteria generally regarded by
legal scholars as necessary elements in a definition of crime
are 1) legal description of an act as socially harmful and 2)
legal provision of a penalty for the act.'[4]

But that definition contains certain ambiguities. First of all,
of course, the state must define crime. In Great Britain, for
example, an offence against the state would be different from
an offence against the state in the Soviet Union. Secondly, in
any society there can be very painful conflicts between what
society perceives to be the greatest good for the greatest
number and the rights of individuals. And thirdly, crimes *by*
the state are generally not clearly defined or subject to
punishment. That is perhaps one reason why Thomas Jefferson, America's ablest Founding Father, advocated a veritable
revolution at least once every generation in order to maintain
democracy's viability. This is also the conflict that prophets of
the Old Testament were talking about: the *cumulative* effect
of individual sin, or corporate sin as it is called, resulting in
society's exploitation of people and a callous disregard of the
needs of human beings, particularly the powerless. Oppression of people was, according to biblical revelation, as much
an offence in God's eyes as the individual acts condemned so
clearly in the Ten Commandments.[5]

We today tend to think of crime only in terms of the
offences of individuals against what is loosely termed the
larger public interest, that is, wrongdoing only as the State
determines it, while in the biblical perspective, sin and crime
are determined by God's Law, and the state may be – indeed,
sometimes is – guilty of breaking it.

In the ministry of Prison Fellowship* we bring mature Christian inmates out of penitentiaries to Washington D.C., for two weeks of intensive Christian discipleship training. In this manner, we have trained over two hundred and fifty inmates, most of whom are deeply committed Christians and all of whom are leaders within their respective institutions. Often we enable them to meet government officials.

One such meeting with several Congressmen a year and a half ago vividly illustrated the difficulty of defining crime. The twelve inmates involved happened all to be women. One of them, named Becky, a round-faced black woman with an irrepressible smile and a warm, gentle spirit, was completing a three-year sentence. During the dialogue, one of the Congressmen asked Becky how someone like her got involved in a life of crime in the first place. She told the story of her life. With nine children and no husband, Becky worked two jobs, doing her level best to stay off welfare.

'We managed, very seldom going hungry,' she related. 'But it was at Christmas, three years ago, that I simply couldn't stand seeing my children without any presents under the tree. All the other kids had presents. Mine didn't. And so I stole. It was wrong. I know it was wrong, but I was doing the best I could and I just couldn't get any presents for my children. It's no excuse, but I stole.'

After Becky finished her story there followed an awkward silence. Finally, a member of Congress walked over, sat down, and put his arm around her.

As we were leaving the meeting, a member of Congress whom I had known for many years – a conservative, and an advocate of stiffer prison penalties for lawbreakers – walked away shaking his head. 'I'm not sure which is the greater crime,' he said wistfully, 'stealing to give your kids a Christmas present or being a Congressman in a society where there is still such economic injustice.' Then he stopped and stared blankly at me. 'You know, every time we pass a law that we know is going to be inflationary, we're taking money out of the pockets of poor people like Becky. I wonder who the bigger criminal is.'

Becky, of course, was in prison; my friend in Congress was not. But the dilemma that Becky's story posed is a very real one: how crime in human society is defined depends on who does the defining.

*For details, see Editor's Note on page 41.

The same problem in America is illustrated again by the celebrated case of the 'Wilmington Ten'. In this case, ten blacks leading a civil rights protest in North Carolina a few years ago were arrested, convicted and sentenced for arson for allegedly burning property during an outburst of racial tension in the state. They all went to prison, correctly so, because the law defined what they did as a crime, and indeed it was a crime. But many Americans are morally offended by the case because what the blacks were protesting against was the undeniable vestige of a hundred years of government-sanctioned racism. Which, then, was the greater crime? One hundred years of government-sanctioned oppression of the powerless or an act of arson? One is chargeable in the courts, and you can be sentenced to prison for it. The other is not defined as a crime simply because it was the way 'society' had acted. The prophets of the Old Testament often spoke on this theme.[5]

Setting terms of punishment can be even more arbitrarily done. For instance, there was a case in America recently of a young man – an alcoholic – who had been in trouble for petty theft a number of times. One day he broke into a neighbour's garage and stole ten dollars' worth of beer. His parents replaced it, but the young man was prosecuted anyway. The judge sentenced him to a minimum of four years and a possible maximum of twenty-five years in prison.[6]

Three years ago, when I visited a maximum security penitentiary in Minnesota, I met a young man who was serving a ten-year sentence for a twenty-dollar unarmed robbery. He, too, was an alcoholic and had been in trouble several times for relatively minor crimes. The judge who sentenced him said he was trying to 'teach him a lesson'. The parole board had denied parole, and the young man faced ten years in one of the darkest, most horrid dungeons in America. Though we managed to get him released after he had served less than two years of his sentence, the wounds of his bruising encounters with the criminal justice system did not quickly heal. Many times we had to steer the young man out of bars or pick him up from some park bench. Finally, last summer, he committed suicide.

The young man was, of course, sick and in need of medical attention. It is true that in his drunken stupor he broke laws. But in my grief over his death, I could not help wondering whether this young man's offence against the state was as grievous a crime as the state's callous treatment of an obviously ill young man.

I offer these examples not because I believe there are easy answers to such perplexing questions, but because I believe it is important in considering the origins of crime – and society's response to it – to be sensitive in defining the problem in the first place.

## Theories about the origins of crime

In the following sections we will examine theories as to the origins of crime that have emerged over the years under four broad headings: 1) psychological, 2) economic, 3) constitutional or physical defects and 4) sociological. We will also examine the findings of one major recent research study and, finally, the Judaeo-Christian view of sin and crime.

### (a) Psychological theories

Charles Goring, English psychiatrist and author of *The English Convict*, which was published in 1913, spent twelve years studying ninety-six character traits of more than three thousand criminals, comparing them with other categories – students, soldiers and those in mental institutions. He concluded that 'feeblemindedness' (that is, limited educational or intellectual capacities) was the single most important correlate of crime. As a result of his widely-publicized study, mental testing of offenders became prevalent. Many other researchers followed Goring's lead, some asserting that sixty to ninety percent of offenders were feebleminded. A year later, in 1914, an American, Henry H. Goddard, presented in a book entitled *Feeblemindedness: Its Causes and Consequences* test results which tended to corroborate Goring's findings.

These theories were shattered after World War One, however, when, as a result of extensive testing in America's prisons, the percentage of 'feeblemindedness' among prison populations was found to be no higher than among the public at large. As testing became more sophisticated, more and more scholars challenged the Goring-Goddard thesis.

In 1936, an American named William Healy published *New Light on Delinquency and Its Treatment*, ably documenting the lack of difference between inmates and the public at large. This has been confirmed yet again in a recent study by the

U.S. Federal Prison population which reveals that eighty-six percent of the inmates had average or better than average IQs (Intelligence Quotients).

Today, many psychiatrists would argue that mental imbalance is a significant cause of crime. And my own experience of living in two prisons and visiting scores of others – spending vast amounts of time with individual inmates – leads me to conclude that the incidence of mental disorder among prisoners is much higher than among the general populace. But that, of course, is predictable, since the experience of imprisonment itself may be psychologically devastating. Then, too, psychiatric disorders are very likely to lead to the types of aberrant conduct which society punishes. Alcoholism, for example, is often associated with psychiatric disorders, and that one factor alone would tend to create a higher percentage of mental imbalance among prisoners since alcohol, as will be discussed later, is such a significant factor in crime.

### (b) Economic theories

W. A. Bonger (1876–1946), a Dutch criminologist, was an early and influential exponent of the theory of economic circumstances as the cause of crime. Holding a fundamentally Marxist world view, he ignored the individual characteristics of the offender, arguing instead that crime is the result of the inequities of the social and economic order in which an acquisitive society encourages aggression and discourages altruism.

A more current Marxist economic critique of crime can be found in a book entitled *Critique of Legal Order: Crime Control in a Capitalistic Society* (1974), authored by Richard Quinney. Quinney asserts that 'criminal law is an instrument . . . to maintain and perpetuate the existing social and economic order.' With socialism, Quinney contends, 'law as we know it' will disappear, for the crime problem will be resolved 'once society has removed all possibility of hatred'.[7] In the perfect view of the Utopian socialist, man would of course be made perfect. There would be no crime, only absolute Utopia. Now, as those of you who know my background will understand very quickly, I am anything but a Marxist. Yet I must say that the Marxist view contains a truth in the point that the injustice of an oppressive society, whether a tyranny of the Left or of the Right, encourages crime. Laws which are unjust, or an economic system which is blatantly unjust, make their impact on society by destroying respect for law and authority.

The prison population of America is predominantly poor and comprised of 'minority' groups. I have come to know many of the inmates very well during the four years we have worked in prisons, and I simply find it hard to believe that all of them would do the kinds of things that they have done if it were not for their bitterness at the injustice they perceived in society, and were it not for the economic pressures and the circumstances in which they lived. Normal temptations are aggravated by the conditions of one's environment.

The conventional liberal view in American politics over the past forty years was expressed very directly by Ramsey Clark, who served as United States Attorney General under President Lyndon Johnson. He said, 'Poverty is *the* cause of crime.' The logical extension of that proposition has very frightening implications. If poverty or racism, which are often linked together, is indeed *the* cause of crime, then society must bear the total burden, and the individual wrongdoer must be excused from responsibility for the consequences of his actions. But is this view correct?

During the blackout in New York City – and by that I refer not to the condition that most Englishmen believe New Yorkers live in continuously, but to a specific twenty-four-hour period in 1977 when electric power failed – there was widespread looting throughout the city. This happens almost every time there is a disaster of this kind in the United States.

President Carter took a classical liberal view of the New York looting: 'Obviously the number one contributing factor to crime of all kinds, in my opinion, is high unemployment among young people, particularly those who are black or Spanish-speaking or in a minority age group where they have such a difficult time getting jobs in times of economic problems.'[8]

Such a statement by the highest official of the government of the United States has the potentially disastrous effect of encouraging the very actions which are so grievous to society because, in effect, he is telling the individual that he is not responsible.

No one publicly took issue with President Carter until about a month later. A study conducted by an official agency in New York City revealed that forty-five percent of those who were arrested for looting had jobs, and that only ten percent were on welfare rolls.[9] Examination of individual incidents of looting further revealed what has been discovered in examining similar cases in almost every other instance; namely that people stole things for which they had absolutely no use or need.

Such findings tend to deflate one of the more popular assumptions of liberalism, namely that crime is an inevitable and almost excusable result of poverty and racism. The faulty logic of such a position was perceptively exposed by Enrico Ferri more than seventy years ago when he wrote:

> If you regard the general condition of misery as the sole cause of criminality, then you cannot get around the difficulty that out of the 1,000 individuals living in misery from the day of their birth to that of their death, only 100 or 200 become criminals . . . If poverty were the sole determining cause, 1,000 out of 1,000 poor ought to become criminals. If only 200 became criminals while 100 commit suicide in their social condition, then poverty alone is not sufficient to explain criminality.[10]

*(c) Constitutional or physical defect theories*
In 1876 an Italian surgeon, Cesare Lombroso expounded in a book entitled *Criminal Man* the superficially appealing thesis that criminals are identifiable by the manifestation of measurable physical characteristics. In other words, if a man looks like a criminal, he must be one. While this seems absurd on its face, it is surprising how many people glibly say, 'He's a criminal: I can tell by his looks,' or, 'He looks like a criminal.' I constantly encounter the public stereotype that all prison inmates are tattooed, scarred, with hairy arms and angry eyes, punched-in noses, with few teeth, and maybe a pair of horns jutting out of the back of their heads! Experiences in our ministry shatter this particularly unfair myth.

When Prison Fellowship began, there were some articles in the Washington newspapers about 'Colson Bringing Convicts to Washington'. Admittedly, that was news, because Washington at that time was shipping a lot of convicts out of the city. But the stir it created in the neighbourhood was unlike anything since the reports of German submarines sighted off the Atlantic coast in World War Two. We were actually threatened with lawsuits because Fellowship House,* a Christian home to which we planned to bring the inmates, is located in a very fashionable section of Washington, surrounded by fine residences and elegant embassies.

The neighbourhood hired an attorney, a legendary figure who was once a close associate of the late President Franklin Roosevelt. One day, he telephoned me. 'Don't you realize what will happen to property values in this neighbourhood if you bring convicts in?' he thundered.

The way we dealt with the problem was to invite neighbourhood residents to our first meeting of inmates at Fellowship House. Whoever happens to be there on any given day is invited to have lunch at a beautiful, polished mahogany table in the large, handsome dining room on the second floor. That first day, the inmates joined those who were at the house for lunch, perhaps thirty in all. The prisoners were dressed in the ordinary clothes with which we had provided them. I stood in the doorway of the dining room with the dissident neighbours and suggested they pick out those in the room who were the convicts: nine of the ten picked a congressman! We have had no difficulty since.

There have been many similar episodes. One illustrates that Christians too can be dupes of the popular stereotype. A group of twelve inmates attended Dr Richard Halverson's Fourth Presbyterian Church in Washington D.C. one Sunday morning. The church was crowded when the convicts arrived, and so they were dispersed through the congregation. One young man, a Filipino-American named Tony who had spent twenty years in prison, sat next to an elderly woman who was wearing a beautiful mink fur stole. While waiting for the service to begin, Tony, who has a charming personality, engaged the woman in conversation. Soon the two were deep in discussion. When Dr Halverson began, he announced that twelve convicts from federal penitentiaries, part of the Prison Fellowship discipleship programme, were visiting the church, and he asked them to stand so they could be welcomed by the other worshippers. As Tony began to rise, the older woman next to him turned to him, held his arm and said, 'Oh no, no, young man, he asked for the convicts to stand up!'

At the turn of the century, Lombroso's writings had a great

*Fellowship House is a place where Christians come from all over the world – pastors, businessmen, lawyers, political officials; in fact many members of Congress meet there for prayer and Bible study.

deal of appeal in almost every country. Today, however, this particular school of thought has very little scientific support. Scientists are, however, still studying the relationships between particular types of criminality and physical abnormalities such as rare chromosome patterns, hormone deficiencies and brain malfunctioning. We do know, from empirical evidence, for example, that very violent people become less violent as they pass the age of forty. Experts are not sure why this is so, but at a certain point the aggressiveness in extremely violent personalities does appear to diminish.

Nevertheless, in none of these detailed and sophisticated scientific investigations has it been shown that crime is a universal result of a particular physical abnormality. As with 'feeblemindedness' and poverty, explanations are far more elusive than they may have seemed at first.


*(d) Sociological theories*
Many sociologists have argued that the primary cause of crime is to be found in an individual's social and environmental influences. The Frenchman, Gabriel Tarde (1843–1904), deduced what he called certain 'laws of imitation'. This is the notion that people are predisposed to commit crimes and are then attracted to criminal activity by the example of others. Hence, a young man living in an area where criminal activity is widespread or perhaps even admired, would imitate that conduct.

It is, in my experience, not an unreasonable proposition. I recall in particular one acquaintance in prison, a hardened criminal who had spent twenty of his thirty-nine years behind bars, much of it on the periphery of serious organized crime. This young man – we will call him Nick – and I were sitting in the prison mess hall, drinking coffee. Our conversation turned to the subject of Nick's religious faith, as he had told me he was a life-long Roman Catholic. I asked him bluntly how he could reconcile killing people with being a Christian. He couldn't, of course; instead, Nick wistfully poured out the story of his life. He grew up, he explained, in a part of New York City, which is known as 'Little Italy' because it is almost entirely populated by first and second generation Italian Americans. 'I never saw no cop until I was twenty,' Nick told me. 'I never knew about any other law than that which my uncles on the block enforced. If ya did wrong, ya was cuffed by one of 'em. They made all the rules. Until I left my neighbourhood, I didn't know there wuz any other law.'

Nick was an altar boy in church; he got his spending money by stealing from the collection plate. Everybody did it, he said: it was one of the benefits of being an altar boy. Then he and an uncle were given a concession stand during one of the festive weekends celebrating a saint's birth. Half of the proceeds went to the church and half went to those who had the concession. The most aggressive young men got the concessions – the clearest mark of success.

In Nick's world, there was permissible stealing and impermissible stealing. The activities of the 'family' – what is popularly known as the Mafia – were always regarded as legitimate, so long as the residents of the immediate community were not the victims. Stealing from others, by extortion, numbers games, rackets, etc., was no different for those who lived in the insular world of 'Little Italy' from the way we today often conduct trade with foreign powers.

Nick's first confrontation with the law outside 'Little Italy' resulted in his arrest and imprisonment, and for the rest of his days he was a marked man. But his value structure – the rights and wrongs of life – were shaped in those twenty years by the traditions of his very self-contained culture.

Nick's story is unfortunately not that unusual. I have met many men in prison whose values were determined by family or local community rather than by the broader dimensions of society. This is particularly the case in rural areas and mountain states. I was in prison with many men who were 'moonshiners', that is, they made liquor in home-made stills. Most couldn't read or write, yet they were God-fearing men, and, as a matter of fact, always carried their Bibles with them. Making whisky is illegal in the U.S. but in their locale it was an honoured profession. They couldn't understand why Federal agents would arrest them and put them in prison. Imprisonment certainly did not deter them, for they would do their time in prison and go right back to making whisky.

One of the most influential American criminologists was Edwin H. Sutherland (1882–1950), a professor at Indiana University. Sutherland's basic thesis was that a person could acquire patterns of lawful behaviour, and that criminal behaviour is learned in association with other persons, particularly within intimate personal groups. He states it this way in his book, *Principles of Criminology*:

> A person becomes delinquent because of an excess of
> definitions favourable to violation of law over definitions
> unfavourable to violation of law . . . When persons
> become criminal, they do so because of contacts with
> criminal patterns and also because of isolation from anti-
> criminal patterns. Any person inevitably assimilates the
> surrounding culture unless other patterns are in con-
> flict.[11]

There is, in my opinion, undeniable validity in this conclusion. Nick, for example, would have provided an excellent
case study for both Tarde and Sutherland. There are, however, three problems with this view.

First, if criminal conduct is encouraged by associations and
environment, then society needs to think very seriously about
the rationale of punishment which puts all known criminals
together in one place. One must think very carefully about the
underlying premise of a prison.

Secondly, like the classic liberal position in America regarding poverty, this point of view comes dangerously close to
removing the individual from all responsibility for his individual decision.

Thirdly, there are simply too many studies which tend to
refute the universality of this view. Another sociologist, for
example, Donald Cressey, discovered that those guilty of
embezzling rarely have anything to do with other criminals.
Dr Samenow, whose work was referred to earlier and will be
discussed again later, studied young adults from the same
family who had been subjected to identical influences. If
environment was the cause, Samenow asked, how could it be
that one became a criminal while his brothers and sisters did
not?

To me, one of the most intriguing and provocative sociological theories of the cause of crime is one put forward by
Robert K. Merton. His theory is especially relevant in the
light of what social critic Tom Wolfe calls the 'me-decade' of
the 1970s, an era permeated by the obsession with self and
egocentricity. Merton believes that high crime rates are a
direct reflection of the values which society places upon individual success, hard work, ambition, and the concept of
getting ahead at all costs. In my country it is heralded as the
great 'American Dream', and is aptly illustrated by my own
rise to the office next to the President of the United States.

Merton argues that the 'dream' is for the most part a myth, and that the legitimate means for getting to the top are not, and indeed cannot, be equally distributed throughout society.

The difficulty is that not everybody in America can realize the dream. Vast numbers of people are virtually condemned to a life of poverty in a ghetto. Therefore they resort to illegitimate means to secure their material goods, and since ends are far more glorified in our society than means, they can often justify what they are doing as consistent with the values of society as they understand them. This culturally-induced success mania exerts a peculiar pressure on the disadvantaged who often see criminal behaviour as the only way to obtain the things which society values so highly.

One need only watch American television to be convinced of the merit of Merton's point. An endless parade of commercials bombard the viewer, exhorting him to indulge his every desire. The commercials, filmed in suburban kitchens or on the grounds of elegant estates, invariably portray upper-middle-class affluence. The poor viewer must constantly be struck by the contrast between his own poverty and the extravagant lifestyle which is advertised as the norm.

John Allen, author of the book *Assault With a Deadly Weapon: The Autobiography of a Street Criminal* (1977) speaks for those who are thus frustrated in our society:

> I really think there is a lot of similarity between the people who live out in the middle-class neighbourhoods and the people I know . . . Everybody wants to have their own joint, own their own home, and have two cars. It's just that we are going about it in a different way. I think keeping up with the Joneses is important everywhere.[12]

In his recent book, *Criminal Violence, Criminal Justice* (1978), Charles E. Silberman, to whom I alluded earlier, makes this observation about the dilemma of the disadvantaged in American society:

> It is harder to be poor in the United States than in most other countries, for American culture has always placed a heavy premium on success (winning is not the main thing; it is the only thing) . . . It should not be surprising that many poor people choose the routes to success that

seem open to them. To youngsters growing up in a lower-class neighbourhood, crime is available as an occupational choice, much as law, medicine, or business management is for adolescents in Palo Alto or Scarsdale, except that lower class youngsters often know a good deal more about the criminal occupations available to them than middle-class youngsters do about their options. In my conversations with young offenders, I was struck by the depth of their knowledge about robbery, burglary, fencing, sale and use of hard and soft drugs, prostitution and pimping, the numbers business, loan sharking and other crimes and rackets. . .

Thus the fabric and texture of life in urban slums and ghettos provide an environment in which opportunities for criminal activity are manifold, and in which rewards for engaging in crime appear to be high – higher than the penalties for crime, and higher than the rewards for avoiding it.[13]

The proliferation of sociological explanations of the cause of crime has produced in recent decades a major shift in examining the origins of criminal behaviour. Attention has moved away from the offender and his personality conflicts and characteristics towards the social processes which have influenced him. The resulting consensus is that criminals themselves are victims of environment, family disintegration, poverty, social conditions, race and education. They are also seen as victims of drugs and alcohol, lack of parental love and care, abuse, and as the products of the warped values they have imitated in others.[14]

*(e) The effects of alcohol and of imprisonment*
There are two other causes of crime which deserve special note; these perhaps would fit into the categories discussed above except for the fact that their importance makes them worthy of special attention.

The first is alcohol. In June, 1978, a special report to the U.S. Congress on Alcohol and Health, compiled by the U.S. Department of Health, Education and Welfare, reported that as many as eighty-three percent of the offenders in prison or jail have some sort of alcohol involvement in their crimes. Whether alcoholism is induced by biological or psychiatric deficiencies, it is generally agreed that it is an illness which must be treated as an illness, and there is no doubt that this particular sickness is a major cause of crime. While I am not a prohibitionist – America's experiment with that proved decidedly unsuccessful – alcoholism must nonetheless be recognized as the epidemic disease it surely is, and its tragic results dealt with.

Secondly, a major cause of crime may be prison itself. As one looks at prison and its effects on the lives of its inhabitants, one sees only a record of absolute failure (see Chapter VI, pp. 152–162). The proof is in the product. According to some estimates, as many as four out of five crimes in America, at least those where the criminal is apprehended, are committed by ex-convicts. The rate of recidivism is staggeringly high in every nation which records and publishes prison statistics.

In 1973 the National Advisory Commission on Criminal Justice Standards and Goals had this to say:

> The failure of major institutions to reduce crimes is incontestable. Recidivism rates are notoriously high. Institutions do succeed in punishing, but they do not deter. They protect the community, but that protection is only temporary. They relieve the community of responsibility by removing the offender, but they make successful reintegration into the community unlikely. They change the committed offender, but the change is more likely to be negative than positive. [15]

Robert Sommer in his book *The End of Imprisonment*, written in 1976, wrote as follows:

> The major justification for another prison book is that the problems remain. Prisons are larger, there are more of them, there is greater violence, higher recidivism, and a rising crime rate outside. The persistence of brutality, the damage to inmates and their families, the lack of useful purpose, and the great amount of time wasted behind bars all suggest that the problems are inherent in the institution. No one has been able to run a decent prison – not the Quakers, not the Soviets, not the conservatives or liberals, not the counties. There is something basically wrong with the idea of forcibly removing

lawbreakers from society, bringing them together in a single location, and placing them under the domination of keepers for long periods.[16]

The very nature of prison, no matter how humane society attempts to make it, produces an environment which inevitably is devastating to its residents.

Gerald Austin McHugh, in his very fine book *Christian Faith and Criminal Justice*, relates an experiment conducted in 1972 at Stanford University. A mock prison was created to test how various individuals would respond to the roles they were asked to play. He writes:

> All participants were college students or professors, and extreme personality types were excluded from the experiment. After only six days (out of a projected fourteen), the experiment had to be stopped because all of those involved, both the keepers and the kept, were suffering severe psychological side-effects. This was simply an experiment, conducted by reasonable, well-educated people who knew that it was only an experiment. It did not even begin to approach the reality of imprisonment as it is known by thousands of human beings in America every day. And yet we believe that such institutions will not serve the purposes of evil, but rather foster the services of good?[17]

Not just prison, but the arbitrariness of the criminal justice system itself, can create such bitterness as to cause further criminal conduct. I remember a very handsome, well-educated young black man I met in prison. I had watched him over a period of weeks and thought him to be one of the bitterest men in the institution. I knew he needed help, and so one night I engaged him in conversation. 'I hope you'll get over your anger. You've got everything going for you when you get out of here,' I told him.

His eyes flashed at me. 'I've got one thing going,' he snarled. 'I'm going to get even.'

Then he told me his story. He had been on parole, had a perfect record, and had been checking in weekly with his probation officer. But one time he made the mistake of crossing a state line without permission. He did so to get married. An angry judge rescinded his parole, and he was back in prison to serve his entire sentence – eighteen months – to its conclusion.

He was studying hard in prison, he explained, listening to other prisoners' stories of how they had been caught. 'Next time, they're not going to catch me,' he grinned defiantly. The obvious unfairness of his treatment had so embittered him, and so disillusioned him with the laws he was being told he must obey, that he was convinced that his only possible response was to break those laws.

Being banished by society and forced to live in subhuman conditions is for many inmates, a number of whom have a very low self-esteem, the ultimate rejection in a lifetime filled with rejection.

This in itself can be a contributing factor to criminal disposition. If a man does not believe that his own life has value, how can he view the lives of others as having value? It thus means nothing to break another's skull. If he cannot love himself, he cannot give or accept love.

There is no better place to learn about crime than in the prisons where so many criminals live. The laws of imitation advanced by Tarde would seem inescapable. There is no more embittering or demeaning environment anywhere, nor one more conducive to encouraging criminal conduct once its residents are released.

*(f) The Samenow and Yochelson research findings*

One of the most recent American investigations into the causes of crime is the Samenow and Yochelson project, recently published in a book entitled *The Criminal Personality*. Their findings are, to say the least, controversial, for they cut across the grain of the sociological and psychiatric theories discussed above.

These two researchers studied the personalities of two hundred and fifty men, spending hundreds of hours with many of them, and as much as eight thousand hours with a few of them. After sixteen years of research, Samenow and Yochelson concluded that they could find no easily definable social or economic factors which could unequivocally be said to cause criminal conduct. Their report exposed the futility of traditional corrective approaches and argued that modern psychological and sociological explanations of crime have served only to buttress the criminal's view of himself as the 'victim' of his own feelings, his family, his environment or his economic status. These theories, Samenow and Yochelson declared, merely offer the criminal more excuses to continue his present way of life.

It should be noted that when Samenow and Yochelson began their research, they themselves held the very conventional view that criminals were merely victims of abuse and deprivation. This is what Samenow wrote:

> People viewed the criminal as somebody who really was a victim of circumstances, if you could just teach him so he could find his way into the mainstream of society. That was all that was necessary. I don't think we quarrelled with much of that, but that turned out not to be the case . . . We found with our people that they rejected the schools and their parents and the responsible forces around them before ever being rejected by them. In other words, they were more victimizers than the victims.[18]

The Samenow-Yochelson study included blacks and whites, grade-school dropouts as well as college graduates, people from the inner city and people from the suburbs, and people from broken homes. Samenow's words suggest some understandable despair: 'We have talked to their families, parents, sisters, brothers – in some cases at great length – as well as studying them. In our search for why they are the way they are, there wasn't anything that stood up.'

The Samenow and Yochelson study places responsibility for criminal behaviour entirely on the criminal himself. Criminals are not crazy or otherwise depraved, or at least no more so than the non-criminal population; they simply prefer to be criminals. The habitual criminal, the study concludes, is a liar and a deceiver. He has little capacity for love, friendship or companionship, and he can commit brutal acts without feelings of guilt, and without his conscience being affected.

Stated simply, Samenow and Yochelson found that criminals are the cause of crime, and not society. Criminal actions are neither a result of racial or economic factors, nor the product of environmental influences or biological aberrations, but rather the result of what criminals think and what they consciously choose to do.

Two widely separated paragraphs from the book make the point:

Perhaps most important is that . . . a criminal is not a victim of circumstances. He makes choices early in life, regardless of his socio-economic status, race or parents' child-rearing practices. A large segment of society has continued to believe that a person becomes a criminal because of environmental influences. Several factors account for the persistence of this conclusion. Parents who have criminal offspring deny that there is something inherent in the individual that surfaces as criminality. They desperately look for a cause and, in the effort to explain, they latch onto some event or series of events in the person's life for which he is not responsible. Many social scientists have a deterministic view of man and for years have been explaining criminality largely in terms of environmental influences. Government programmes have operated on this basis. The media have espoused this attitude . . . Changing the environment does not change the man. Finally the criminal is ever ready to present himself as a victim once he is apprehended. He feeds society what he at best only half believes himself. Actually, he knows that circumstances have nothing to do with his violence, but he uses that rhetoric if he thinks it will lead others to view him more sympathetically. . .

. . . All specific criminal acts are programmed in the thinking of the criminal. Impulse and compulsion imply loss of control. But all his life the criminal has been calculating, scheming, and controlling. His behaviour may appear to be impulsive, or compulsive, because it is sudden to the observer. In no case has impulse or compulsion held up. A pattern of criminal thinking has preceded the crime in question. The idea may have been considered, but rejected, many times before. The crime occurs after deterrents have corroded and have been cut off. When a specific crime such as assault has not been planned in advance, it is a matter of a criminal's responding in a habitual manner. He still maintains control of his behaviour. All of us are habituated to doing something in a specific way, such as driving an automobile; but we maintain control over what we do. To say that a pattern is ingrained in an individual does not diminish personal responsibility or decision-making capacity. To avoid a penalty, the criminal may try to convince others that he acted impulsively. What has been so striking and consistent is that, to a man, our criminals have eventually revealed to us that what they did was an exercise of choice. In fact, because of our procedures, it was demeaning to them to deny the role of choice.[19]

While I acknowledge much of what Samenow and Yochelson found – and substantially agree with their suggested remedy (see page 38 below) – I am deeply concerned that the widespread publication of their findings will cause an already calloused public to become even more insensitive to the needs of those who are incarcerated. It would be tragic if the excellent scholarship of the Samenow-Yochelson Report were simply to result in a reinforcement of biases and stereotypes already so widely held.

*(g) The Judaeo-Christian view*
All the schools of thoughts so far considered, with the exception of Samenow and Yochelson, proceed from the basic assumption that man is either good or at least morally neutral. Evil actions performed by man are viewed as a result of environmental and social conditions, or as aberrations from the norm of one kind or another. Man is basically good and therefore has a perfectible nature. The Judaeo-Christian tradition, by contrast, represents the exact opposite of this popular presupposition.

Dr J. I. Packer, whose writings are known to many Christians in Britain and America, in his book *Knowing God* aptly describes modern man's view of himself and how this clashes with the biblical view:

> Modern man, conscious of his tremendous scientific achievements in recent years, naturally inclines to a high opinion of himself. He views material wealth as in any case more important than moral character, and in the moral realm he is resolutely kind to himself, treating small virtues as compensating for great vices and refusing to take seriously the idea that, morally speaking, there is anything much wrong with him. He tends to dismiss a bad conscience, in himself as in others, as an unhealthy psychological freak, a sign of disease and mental aberration rather than an index of moral reality.
>
> Modern man is convinced that, despite all his little peccadilloes – drinking, gambling, reckless driving,

'fiddling,' black and white lies, sharp practice in trading, dirty reading, and what have you – he is at heart a thoroughly good fellow. Then, as pagans do (and modern man's heart is pagan – make no mistake about that), he imagines God as a magnified image of himself, and assumes that God shares his own complacency about himself. The thought of himself as a creature fallen from God's image, a rebel against God's rule, guilty and unclean in God's sight, fit only for God's condemnation, never enters his head. [20]

The Judaeo-Christian perspective is based upon biblical revelation. Man was created perfect, in the image of God, but he was given a free will, and one of his first free acts was to disobey God. That act of disobedience, that alienation from his Creator, was the original sin of which all mankind is now heir. Man falls short of the glory of God (Romans 3:23), and his heart is depraved (Mark 7:20–23). He continues to live in revolt and rebellion against God, and therefore at enmity with God's creations – his own neighbours and even himself. While man is capable of good, he remains a sinner, and the essence of sin is the love of self over against the love of God. Excessive self-love leads to pride, lawlessness, unrighteousness, transgressions and evil. Man's self is exalted against God's will. That is egotism – and sin.

C. H. McIntosh, an English scholar of a century ago whose commentaries continue to be read widely today, succinctly summed it up:

> Man spoils everything. Place him in a position of highest dignity and he will degrade himself. Endow him with the most ample privileges and he will abuse them; scatter blessings around him in richest profusion and he will prove ungrateful; place him in the midst of the most impressive institutions and he will corrupt them. Such is man. Such is his nature in its fairest forms and under the most favourable circumstances. [21]

Crime can be said to be one of the manifestations of man's sinful nature, which can be traced back to Adam. One of the most perceptive exposures of sinful nature is found in Augustine's *Confessions*:

. . . I willed to commit theft, and I did so, not because I was driven to it by any need, unless it were by poverty of justice, and dislike of it, and by a glut of evildoing. For I stole a thing of which I had plenty of my own and of much better quality. Nor did I wish to enjoy that thing which I desired to gain by theft, but rather to enjoy the actual theft and the sin of theft.

In a garden nearby to our vineyard there was a pear tree, loaded with fruit that was desirable neither in appearance nor in taste. Late one night – to which hours according to our pestilential custom we had kept up our street games – a group of very bad youngsters set out to shake down and rob this tree. We took great loads of fruit from it, not for our own eating, but rather to throw it to the pigs; even if we did eat a little of it, we did this to do what pleased us for the reason that it was forbidden.

Behold my heart, O Lord, behold my heart upon which you had mercy in the depths of the pit. Behold, now let my heart tell you what it looked for there, that I should be evil without purpose and that there should be no cause for my evil but evil itself. Foul was the evil, and I loved it. [22]

Some modern scholars mock Augustine. Here, they say, is a man who was a philanderer and a heavy drinker. Surely he could think of more heinous sins than stealing a few pears from a neighbour's tree. But they miss the point entirely. The fruit, Augustine wrote, 'was desirable neither in appearance nor in taste'. Man sins, Augustine believed, not because of outside influences or factors beyond his controls, nor even to satisfy his own needs or desires, but simply because he *chooses* to sin. In the classical Christian view, each individual is responsible for his own sin, which is why repentance is essential to true conversion.

**Conclusion**
In my own experience, each of the explanations of why people commit crime discussed above has some validity, but no single theory has a monopoly of the truth. As Lord Longford concluded after a two-year study of crime in this country some years ago, 'There are as many causes of crime as there are criminals.'

Though I believe that crime is generally the result of a conscious and deliberate decision, and therefore originates in the very nature of man, it is nonetheless nurtured by a complex root structure which reaches deep within the soil of our society. Take, for example, 'Nick', the Italian-American inmate whom I described earlier. He told me one night that he had deliberately chosen his criminal occupation, which was trafficking in narcotics. I asked him how he could be so foolish. He was arrested in New York State, which imposes a mandatory life sentence for conviction of serious narcotics offences.

Nick's reply said a lot, not only about Nick but about others like him: 'Jeez, Chuck, you gotta remember,' he said, 'that I used to work as a rod carrier in the construction gangs. I was paid $18 an hour, carrying rods on the eightieth floor of the World Trade Center. One slip and I'd be a gonner for sure. So for $18 I risked my life. I could make $300,000 in one week selling heroin, and if I got caught, that's only life imprisonment.'

So long as crime pays and the criminal is willing to pay the overhead, there will always be plenty of Nicks who make coldly calculated decisions to do what they choose to do.

Poverty, racism and oppression cannot be dismissed as origins of crime. They are aggravating causes. I have interviewed too many people in prison who are poor not to believe that this is so. I will never forget, for example, what an inmate said to me one day: 'You don't think you could ever be here, do you?' The community volunteer next to me shook his head. The inmate said, 'Just remember, you're only nine meals away from being a criminal. When you see your child's stomach bloating, remember you could be here where I am.' People rarely starve in our Western society. There are other things to do than steal. But nonetheless the point is one which all must take to heart.

I am also convinced that our culture shapes our values. The affluent age in which we live encourages people to believe that they are entitled, as a matter of right, to the so-called good things of life, and this implies getting them any way they can. Our egocentric age makes self-gratification the prime object of life; hence absolute standards and laws have little relevance. The harsh and strident voices of our culture which exalt material success and achievement – the 'do-your-own-thing' promoters – drown the few and feeble voices of moral rectitude and of the absolutes of right and wrong.

As Malcolm Muggeridge argued so compellingly in the 1976 London Lectures,[23] a primary villain in this trend is television. For millions, reality is what appears night after night on the box. It is a vicious cycle. Dramas which portray gang violence do not merely reflect actual gang violence, they encourage it. Programmes which dignify immorality encourage immorality. What we see played before our eyes in the theatre of television is, or rapidly becomes, a mirror of ourselves.

Then, too, I believe that what society naïvely regards as the cure of crime can itself be a cause. Prison environments are a proven breeding ground for criminal behaviour. Alcohol and drug addiction are also demonstrated causes of crime.

Still, at the heart of it, crime is man's own moral choice. Samenow and Yochelson are, in my opinion, correct. Their research findings and St Augustine's story are consistent with the Judaeo-Christian perspective of man and sin.

While this recognition of our fundamentally flawed nature might seem over-pessimistic, it is not. In our teaching in the prisons, we of Prison Fellowship emphasize individual self-worth. Man is, after all, created in the image of God, and therefore, God intends that his attributes of righteousness and holiness should be our attributes. We have witnessed astonishing results when men and women grasp this concept and discover a standard of value and worth they want to live up to.

If mankind has a disposition to sin, the key question is how is righteousness to be achieved?

Samenow and Yochelson say that it must come from the 'deliberate conversion of the offender to a more responsible lifestyle'. I agree. But the question is still unanswered: what makes the offender want to change? What causes 'conversion', a term which both Christians and Samenow and Yochelson use?

One illustration of hundreds that I might give may help to answer the question:

I was recently in a prison in North Carolina, taking part in a seminar for fifty inmates.* After an evening meeting, one of the inmates asked to see me alone. He was tough-looking. It wouldn't have taken a disciple of Lombroso to pick him out of the crowd! His black hair was shaved close, his face scarred,

---

*Another aspect of the Prison Fellowship ministry involves taking teaching teams inside prisons for a full week's course.

his eyes piercing. From his muscular body I knew that he had spent hours in the prison weightlifting room, which is the chief recreation of many inmates, who strive to prove their macho toughness. But there was also a hurt and pleading look in his eyes. He said to me, 'I want what you have, but I know I can't have it. I want to do good but I do bad.' STEP ONE: He wanted something better, a standard of value and worth he could live up to.

It turned out that he was the leader in the prison, the toughest of the convicts, the one who led every inmate uprising, the one regarded by the prison staff as the chief trouble-maker.

The young man then told me his life story. Having been in institutions for twenty-two of his twenty-five years, his earliest memories were of an orphanage. He did not know who his father and mother were. Every time he was released from institutional custody he was in trouble and was immediately returned. He had one sister but, as he told me, whenever he visited the town she lived in, she notified the police and had him arrested. He had no friends, little education, and a totally depraved view of himself and of society. He had been convicted of very serious crimes, and frankly admitted that when released he would undoubtedly commit more.

As I looked into the man's eyes, I could not help wondering what possible hope there would be for him. He was imprisoned at a cost to society of twenty thousand dollars a year. Yet letting him out on the street would be a clear and present danger to law-abiding citizens. What could conceivably be done with a man like this?

I told him what it really meant to be a Christian, but I wondered how in the world that would penetrate his mind and heart, so low was his view of himself and so convinced was he of his own evil. We had a long talk that night, long enough for me to realize that the man was genuinely seeking something better for his life.

Later that week, at the conclusion of our seminar, our Prison Fellowship instructor invited all those who wished to make decisions for Christ to step forward. That is all we ever do, a simple invitation involving no pressure or coercion. Every eye in the room turned to this inmate, for he was the leader. Slowly he got up out of his chair and walked forward. When he did, thirty men followed him. STEP TWO: He made a decision.

I have since received from that inmate some of the most remarkable letters I have ever read. The man is studying, growing as a disciple of Christ, being helped by the community, and leading others in prison in Bible study. STEP THREE: He is seriously seeking a deeper relationship with Christ, studying and being helped to understand the values of the kingdom of God.

He will be released from prison next year. I don't know what will happen to him. We will help him, because Christ commands us to do so. Whether we succeed or fail, that is the command laid upon us. We do it to satisfy our Lord, not statisticians.

Maybe he'll make it; maybe he won't. I think he will. And if he does, I can assure you that the man will have found redemption in the only conceivable way it is to be found.

That, of course, is the essence of what we Christians call 'the Good News'. It is indeed good news, because we believe that through faith in Jesus Christ, we are made righteous before God. We believe further, as Scripture says, that when a man is in Christ, he is a new creation.

I hasten to add that authentic redemption is not as simple as some Christians would make it seem. Sometimes in our Christian literature and preaching we make conversion seem like instant sanctification, as if simply at the name 'Jesus' and at the snapping of one's fingers a person is converted from a hardened criminal into a saint. It just doesn't work like that. The truth is that conversion may occur in an instant, but the process of coming from sinfulness into a new life can be a long and arduous journey.

But the fact is that it does happen. I have seen it happen over and over again in prison after prison, many too many times to doubt its validity.

It is perhaps ironic that the harder we search for scientific answers to the questions of human behaviour, the more elusive those answers become. And yet, an agreement that there are no easy laboratory-provable answers to the mysteries of human behaviour may be the beginning of wisdom. For as each new theory, at first so promising, proves as futile as the last, a human being cries out in frustration for help. *There* is the delightful irony: for only when he does that can he find the One who can indeed redeem him.

**Editor's Note: The work of Prison Fellowship**

Prison Fellowship grew out of the experiences of Chuck Colson during his seven months' prison sentence in federal penitentiaries in the United States. He had been convicted for 'disseminating information to the media about a defendant awaiting trial'. On his release early in 1975 he sought and obtained permission for selected prisoners to be temporarily released in order to attend Christian discipleship seminars in Washington D.C. This led to the holding of a series of such seminars in and outside other American prisons and to the formation of Prison Fellowship in the summer of 1976.

Prison Fellowship is an interdenominational body, now has a staff of over 30, and concentrates on four main areas of ministry:

1. Discipleship seminars held in Washington
2. In-prison discipleship seminars
3. Chaplaincy services to certain prisons
4. A service to link prisoners with volunteers from local churches

Chuck Colson has spoken about the work of the Fellowship in many parts of the world. He has also described its development in his books *Born Again* and *Life Sentence*.

Mr Colson and some of his colleagues from the Fellowship have been involved in an advisory capacity in the formation of the Prison Christian Fellowship in England in 1978/9.

Fuller details of the rapidly developing and important work of both Fellowships can be obtained from the following addresses:

Prison Fellowship, Box 40562, Washington D.C. 20016, U.S.A.

Prison Christian Fellowship, Box 263, London SW1.

# Notes and References

1 Stanton Samenow and Samuel Yochelson, *The Criminal Personality* (J. Aronsun, New York, 1977).
2 Charles E. Silberman, *Criminal Violence, Criminal Justice* (New York, 1978), p. 4.
3 Sir Leon Radzinowicz and Joan King, *The Growth of Crime* (Hamish Hamilton, 1977), quoted in Silberman, pp. 5–6.
4 Edwin H. Sutherland, *White Collar Crime* (New York, 1949), quoted in Richard Quinney, *The Problem of Crime* (Harper & Row, 1977), pp. 4–5.
5 See, for example, Amos 2 and Isaiah 2.
6 'Indeterminate' sentences of imprisonment are frequently allowed under American penal codes. The court specifies a minimum and a maximum length. But the length of time actually served is decided by prison authorities during the course of the sentence.
7 Richard Quinney, *Critique of Legal Order: Crime Control in a Capitalist Society* (Boston, 1974), quoted in Ernest van den Haag, 'No Excuse for Crime', *The Annals of the American Academy* January, 1976, pp. 137–138.
8 Jimmy Carter, 'Interview with the National Black Network', *Weekly Compilation of Presidential Documents*, July, 1977.
9 Criminal Justice Agency, Inc., New York City, August 14, 1977.
10 Enrico Ferri, *The Positive School of Criminology* (Chicago, 1906), quoted in Ernest van den Haag, *Punishing Criminals* (New York, 1975), pp. 102–103.
11 Edwin H. Sutherland and Donald R. Cressey, *Principles of Criminology* (Philadelphia, 1955), quoted in Harry Elmer Barnes and Negley K. Teeters, *New Horizons in Criminology* (New Jersey, 1959), p. 159.
12 John Allen, *Assault with a Deadly Weapon: The Autobiography of a Street Criminal* (New York, 1977), quoted in Silberman, p. 87.
13 Silberman, pp. 89–90.
14 From an English perspective, there is a valuable discussion of the research evidence as to the relationships between these factors and criminality in Michael Rutter and Nicola Madge, *Cycles of Disadvantage* (Heinemann Educational, London 1976).
15 *The National Advisory Commission on Criminal Justice Standards and Goals*, 1973, quoted in Gerald Austin McHugh, *Christian Faith and Criminal Justice* (New York, 1978), pp. 66–67.
16 R. Sommer, *The End of Imprisonment* (Oxford University Press, New York, 1976).

17  *New York Times Magazine* (April 8, 1973), p. 38, quoted in McHugh, p. 180.
18  *Psychology Today* (February, 1978), p. 89.
19  Stanton Samenow and Samuel Yochelson, *The Criminal Personality* (J. Aronsun, New York, 1977), quoted in *The Federal Bar Journal*, Vol. 35, Summer–Fall 1976, p. 240.
20  J. I. Packer, *Knowing God* (Hodder & Stoughton, 1973), pp. 117–118.
21  C. H. McIntosh, *Genesis To Deuteronomy* (Loizeaux Bros., 1972), p.343.
22  *The Confessions of St. Augustine* (New York, 1960), pp. 69–70.
23  Malcolm Muggeridge, *Christ and the Media* (Hodder & Stoughton, London, and Eerdmans, Grand Rapids, 1977).

## II Criminal Sanctions

Sir Norman Anderson

**Introduction**
If anyone imagines for a moment that the subject of criminal sanctions is simple – or, indeed, that it is not shot through with complexities, anomalies and contradictions – he must be exceedingly naïve. It is true that all the 'classical' theories about the purpose and justification of criminal punishment still stand, and that none of them can properly, as I see it, be written off as obsolete or outmoded; but the questions of how they should be put into practice, to what extent they are effective, and whether they are not – to some degree, at least – mutually incompatible or even contradictory, remain problems to which no human mind has yet found any wholly satisfactory answer.

Since my contribution is part of a series relating to 'Contemporary Christianity', I shall begin with the basic difference of opinion between most Christians, on the one side, and many humanists, on the other, regarding the fundamental aim or justification of punishment in general, and of criminal sanctions in particular. To illustrate this, I propose to quote somewhat extensively from the writings of Professor H. L. A. Hart[1] (as an outstandingly lucid legal philosopher who is a serious moralist but emphatically not a Christian) and to compare them with the teaching of the Bible. After that, I shall go on to consider a number of detailed practical problems – of which, of course, periodical mention will be made throughout the course of this chapter.

The complexity of the whole question of criminal sanctions is well illustrated by the fact that Hart felt it necessary, some years ago, to write an essay

to provide a framework for the discussion of the mounting perplexities which now surround the institution of criminal punishment, and to show that any morally tolerable account of this institution must exhibit it as a compromise between distinct and partly conflicting principles.[2]

We must beware, he insisted, of our desire for an 'over-simplification of multiple issues which require separate consideration', and we must realise that

> what is most needed is *not* the simple admission that instead of a single value or aim (Deterrence, Retribution, Reform or any other) a plurality of different values and aims should be given as a conjunctive answer to some *single* question concerning the justification of punishment. What is needed is the realization that different principles (each of which may in a sense be called a 'justification') are relevant at different points in any morally acceptable account of punishment. What we should look for are answers to a number of different questions such as: What justifies the general practice of punishment? To whom may punishment be applied? How severely may we punish? In dealing with these and other questions concerning punishment we should bear in mind that in this, as in most other social institutions, the pursuit of one aim may be qualified by or provide an opportunity, not to be missed, for the pursuit of others.[3]

## Common justifications for punishment

### (a) Deterrence

Let us begin, then, with a brief review of those grounds which are most commonly advanced as a justification for punishment. In the case of criminal sanctions deterrence (that is, of the offender himself from any repetition of his offence, or – more generally – of others from similar actions) would, I think, head most people's list. This can be seen, for example, in the long and continuing debate in this country about whether the death penalty should, or should not, be re-introduced as the ultimate sanction for murder, on the ground that it 'stands to reason' that it represents a uniquely effective deterrent (see further below, p. 55f.); and it can also be seen in the steps taken, or contemplated, today in several Muslim countries to re-introduce some of the savage corporal punish-

ments prescribed by Islamic law for a few precisely defined
(*hadd*) offences (see Additional Note p. 66).

It would, I think, even be true to say that a few Utilitarians
(i.e. those who hold that the greatest happiness of the greatest
possible number should be the sole criterion for public action)
would probably regard deterrence as the sole basic justification for punishment, on the principle that the infliction of
pain on some can be contemplated only in the interests of the
greater good of the community as a whole. But it is exceedingly difficult to maintain what might be described as a purely
utilitarian approach to this subject. It is, of course, perfectly
possible to argue that the very young, the mentally deficient,
or those whose offences were committed by mistake, acciden-
tally or under extreme duress, should be exempted from
punishment on the ground that in their case no threat of
punishment would serve any useful purpose. Even this argument loses some of its force in the face of the counter-
argument that to open the door to any exception or excuse
might tend to weaken the deterrent effect of the threat of
punishment on the community at large, or at least on certain
individuals, whereas the *infliction* (as opposed to the threat)
of punishment even on those who cannot be regarded as
'criminally responsible' might have a considerable social
impact. But this counter-argument could also be used in
extreme cases to justify the punishment of the totally
innocent – or, indeed, the use of torture or forms of punishment which the great majority of people today would regard
as cruel and inhuman – and there are very few Utilitarians
who would go so far as this.

It is, however, fair to ask them *why* it is that they would
draw the line at punishing the innocent or those who are not
'criminally responsible' – or, indeed, at torture or any punishment which is out of all proportion in its severity to the offence
that has been committed. The answer of the extreme Utilitarian would probably be that any such action would so
greatly upset the public conscience – as 'unfair', 'unjust' or
cruel – that it might lead to the breakdown or overthrow of
the whole system. And so it might. But Hart is surely right
when he observes that it is important to emphasize that in such
cases 'there are moral objections (at least as firm as any
utilitarian principles) to punishing persons who are clearly
undeterrable' (because they are incapable of making any
effective choice), and that

these objections are not merely subordinate aspects of the social desirability of avoiding public excitement and nullification of the system, etc. Indeed the reason why we should expect 'public excitement' or the nullification of a system which permitted 'the undeterrables' to be executed is precisely because it is widely considered (independently of social welfare) *unfair* or *unjust* to punish them. A theory of punishment which disregarded these moral convictions or viewed them simply as factors, frustration of which made for socially undesirable excitement, is a different kind of theory from one which *out of deference to those convictions themselves* restricts punishment to those who are deterrable or capable of acting so as to avoid punishment.[4]

All the same, Hart insists that 'there is a coherent answer which a cautious Utilitarian can make to this objection without admitting notions of retribution, unless "retribution" means merely that punishment must be confined to those who have broken the law and could have helped this.' But he emphasizes that

the utilitarian position, to be plausible, must be regarded as . . . fixing a *maximum* beyond which punishment is not justified. The utilitarian position, in however sophisticated a version, cannot plausibly be regarded as something which we can use in an unqualified fashion. There are many different ways in which we think it morally incumbent on us to *qualify* or *limit* the pursuit of the utilitarian goal by the methods of punishment. Some punishments are ruled out as too barbarous or horrible to be used whatever their social utility; we also limit punishments in order to maintain a scale for different offences which reflects, albeit very roughly, the distinction felt between the moral gravity of these offences. Thus we make some approximation to the ideal of justice by treating morally like cases alike and morally different ones differently.[5]

Hart is still more emphatic, of course, in his disapproval of the punishment of the innocent – again on moral grounds. But he stops short of saying that any given form of wrong-doing deserves any specific retributive response.

## (b) Reformation

Many other people today would opt for the reform of the criminal as the primary aim of penal sanctions – and the earnest desire for such reform is naturally shared by Christians and humanists alike – both in the interests of the offenders themselves and of the community to which they belong. There are, indeed, a few people who profess to believe that crime is always and only a symptom of some disease.[6] If this were so the term 'punishment' would, strictly speaking, be inappropriate for the treatment to which offenders should be subjected; and the word 'cure' should be substituted for 'reform'. There can be no manner of doubt that some offenders are, in fact, suffering from some disease of mind or body and are in urgent need of medical assistance – to say nothing of the far greater number whose moral guilt is considerably lessened by reason of 'diminished responsibility'. But it is a far cry from this to suggest that the generality of criminals are not reasonably normal human beings who are morally responsible – in varying degrees – for what they do.[7] And much the same attitude towards moral responsibility should, I think, logically be taken up by those convinced 'determinists' who believe that no offender could have acted in any way other than he did.

There are comparatively few people, however, whose philosophical determinism is such as to lead them to this conclusion. Nor, in my opinion, can the thesis that crime is always a symptom of disease stand up to serious challenge. There are many offenders who know perfectly well that they are breaking the law, and who deliberately decide to do so – whether for financial gain, frustration, rebellion against the very structure of society, lust, or a multitude of other reasons. Nor will the Christian readily accede to the view that anyone is beyond divine redemption. In this context, however, we are not concerned so much with radical redemption, which Chuck Colson has already discussed (Chapter I, pp. 38–40), as with such reformation of character as will enable the offender to resume his place as a reasonably responsible and trustworthy citizen. But how is this to be achieved? There can be no doubt, I think, that a warning from the police, an appearance in court, a probation order or a suspended prison sentence will often have considerable effect; and in more extreme circumstances a short period in prison may serve to provide the necessary shock.[8] But experience has shown that the hope that a number of years in prison, borstal or some similar institution has much chance of leading to moral reform is sanguine in the extreme (see also Chapter VI, pp. 152–162). It does sometimes happen, thank God; but the fact remains that prisoners usually seem to succumb to the deadening influence of prison routine, or to become cynical and hardened through their contact with other, and more experienced, criminals. Our prisons are, moreover, so overcrowded today (when the average prison population in England and Wales has risen, it seems, from some 33,000 in 1965–69 to 41,500 in 1977), so understaffed, and so generally inadequate, that it has recently been stated that 'in some cases even relatively modern buildings might be described as "penal slums".' In such conditions moral reform becomes less and less likely – and any feasible alternative to a custodial sentence deserves the most urgent and sympathetic consideration. Where accused persons *must* be remanded in custody, moreover, this should be in strict segregation from those who have been sentenced; and it seems to me that *all* custodial sentences should be kept as short as circumstances allow.

There is plenty of scope for discussion about the sort of régime which should, ideally, be provided in prisons or similar institutions. The major deprivations prisoners suffer are, obviously, the loss of their freedom and their separation from their families and friends. There is also, in many cases, anxiety about their wives, their children and their future. Overcrowding, insanitary conditions, or anything which detracts from basic human dignity can never be right in principle, although the very concept of prison as a form of punishment may well indicate a certain degree of acceptable austerity. This should certainly be mitigated in the case of those who have completed their period of *penal* incarceration, but will have to be kept in custody indefinitely because of t' ᵴ danger[9] to which their release might expose the public (oɩ some section of the public). For the rest, it is vital that prisoners' eyes should be continually directed to the time when they will be allowed to return to ordinary life; and both the training they receive and the work they do should be designed to contribute to their eventual rehabilitation. A salient problem, however, is that individuals react in such very different ways to the same circumstances and environment. What one man will accept as his just deserts, and respond to accordingly, will eat into the heart of another as an example of an injustice which will fester into a bitter resentment against society as a whole.

It should be added that those who would put deterrence above reform as the basic aim or justification of punishment would agree with a great deal of what has just been said. Deterrence and reform are far from being of necessity antithetical or mutually exclusive, and I would reiterate Professor Hart's view that, in questions about punishment, 'we should bear in mind that . . . the pursuit of one aim may be qualified by or provide an opportunity, not to be missed, for the pursuit of others.'

### (c) Retribution

Where I disagree with Hart is in his repudiation of any 'retributive' element as a legitimate component – let alone as the basic justification – in an acceptable view of the aims and rationale of punishment. I realize, of course, that my own views on this subject are greatly influenced by my religious convictions, just as Hart's are by his atheism. Hart does, however, accept the principle (which he terms 'Retribution in Distribution') that punishment is appropriate *only* in the case of a person who has in fact committed an offence, and that it should bear some relation to the gravity of what he has done. But as soon as this is accepted, however, it is difficult completely to repudiate any concept whatever of what he calls 'Retribution as a General Justifying Aim' of punishment – even if only in a secondary capacity. Manifestly, there is a genuine difference between 'distribution' and 'aim' which Hart rightly notes; but to hold that only those who have actually committed a crime may be punished, that the punishment should correspond, as closely as possible, to the 'gravity of their offences', and that excessive or inappropriate punishments should be regarded as 'unfair' or 'unjust', seems to come very close to postulating that the offender should never receive a punishment greater than he *deserves*. And as soon as we begin to use terms such as 'deserves' or 'deserts' (which Hart, so far as I can remember, studiously avoids, presumably for this very reason), we almost inevitably become involved in that element of retribution which, as I see it, is virtually inherent in any concept of justice as such.

### The biblical approach to the problem of punishment

At this point I think I should outline what I believe to be the biblical approach to the problem of punishment in general, before returning to a more detailed discussion of the way in which, and degree to which, effect can (or should) be given to this by the State in its criminal jurisdiction.

*(a) God's attitude to sin*

In this context we must necessarily start with the character of God himself, as this is portrayed in both the Old and the New Testaments. As early as Exodus 34:6 he is described as a 'compassionate and gracious God, slow to anger, abounding in love and faithfulness, maintaining love to thousands, and forgiving wickedness, rebellion and sin'. But it is also explicitly added that 'he does not leave the wicked unpunished'. In the New Testament, moreover, we find precisely the same emphasis when John sums up the character of God in the two sublime statements that 'God is love'[10] and 'God is light'[11] – statements which he amplifies by telling us, in regard to the first, that 'this is how God showed his love among us: he sent his one and only Son into the world that we might live through him'; and, in the second, by adding that 'in him is no darkness [that is, moral evil] at all'.

The fundamental basis of just retribution is unequivocally expressed in verses like Galatians 6:7 and 8, where the Galatians were exhorted: 'Do not be deceived: God cannot be mocked. A man reaps what he sows. The one who sows to his sinful nature will from that nature reap destruction; the one who sows to please the Spirit, from the Spirit will reap eternal life.' Similarly, Hebrews 2:2 speaks of 'every violation or disobedience' (that is, transgression of the law by positive act or negative omission) receiving 'its just punishment'. Elsewhere it is, of course, made clear that, when a person turns to God in repentance and faith, his sins will not only be forgiven but even 'forgotten', and fellowship with God will immediately be established or restored. Further, in some cases we are told, in figurative language, that God will 'restore' (or 'pay him back for') the years that the locusts have eaten,[12] while in other cases the results even of forgiven sins will remain. An example of this is the fact that David, when he confessed his sin against Uriah and Bathsheba, was fully restored to fellowship with the God to whom he had made his heartfelt confession,[13] but the family repercussions resulting from his sin continued to trouble him.

The punishment for sin of which the Bible speaks may certainly, therefore, be termed retribution, provided only that that word is not understood as carrying any overtones of revenge, spite or vindictiveness; for there is no antithesis between God's condemnation of sin and his love for the sinner. On the contrary, the one is the obverse side of the other, for he can truly be said to 'hate' what causes spiritual injury to those whom he loves. Very often, therefore, the motive for his punishments is primarily *disciplinary*, as we learn from Hebrews 12:5 and 6, where a passage from Proverbs is quoted as:

> My son, do not make light of the Lord's discipline,
>     and do not lose heart when he rebukes you,
> because the Lord disciplines those he loves,
>     and he punishes everyone he accepts as a son.[14]

We are also told that, while our fathers disciplined us for a while as they thought best,

> God disciplines us for our good, that we may share in his holiness. No discipline seems pleasant at the time, but painful. Later on, however, it produces a harvest of righteousness and peace for those who have been trained by it.[15]

Equally, there are many examples in the Bible of God using punishment, or the threat of punishment, to *deter* men from evil. An outstanding instance of this can be found in Deuteronomy 28, where a list of blessings which will result from obedience is followed by a corresponding catalogue of the curses which disobedience may entail. Such judgments are sometimes visited on human beings in this life, while others are reserved for the bar of eternity – at which perfect records are available. If they persist in evil and finally reject God's free offer of forgiveness and eternal life – provided for them at infinite cost – the divine judgment is equally eternal or irreversible;[16] and it is significant to note that the most outspoken warnings of this are recorded as coming from the lips of Christ himself.[17]

Another point of cardinal importance is that the judgment of God is always completely just. He alone knows *all* the facts; for 'nothing in all creation is hidden from God's sight. Everything is uncovered and laid bare before the eyes of him to whom we must give account.'[18] This applies not only to the precise details of some concrete offence, but also to all our thoughts, motives and past experiences, for his word 'penetrates even to dividing soul and spirit, joints and marrow; it judges the thoughts and attitudes of the heart'.[19] He alone can (and does) sort out all our mixed motives; he knows just how much pressure and temptation each of us can withstand; and he gives full weight to every factor of heredity, environment, and immediate circumstance. From one point of view this is, indeed, an awesome thought; but from another it is a source of deep comfort. 'I know, O Lord, that your laws are righteous, and in faithfulness you have afflicted me.'[20]

*(b) The role of human authority*
Such, then, is the judgment of God himself. But he has not only created us as individuals; he has also set us in families, communities and nations. Indeed, the very institution of human governments and secular authorities is part of his plan for his world;[21] and we are specifically told that such are 'sent by him to punish those who do wrong and to commend those who do right'.[22] At the same time, every human exercise of authority, and every judgment of man on man, is inevitably prone to ignorance, error, bias and even tyranny; it is always subordinate and limited in its scope; and those who exercise it – whether in the promulgation of legislation, the decisions of executive discretion or the deliberations of the courts – all alike stand under the judgment of God himself. It is the duty of rulers to 'hold no terror for those who do right, but [only] for those who do wrong', St Paul insists; and he continues:

> Do you want to be free from fear of the one who is in authority? Then do what is right and he will commend you. For he is God's servant to do you good. But if you do wrong, be afraid, for he does not bear the sword for nothing. He is God's servant, an angel of justice to bring punishment on the wrongdoer.[23]

Now it seems clear that this gives ample, though strictly delegated, authority to governments – legislature, executive and judiciary alike – to maintain law and order. We are, indeed, specifically commanded to pray for 'kings, and all those in authority, that we may lead peaceful and quiet lives in all godliness and holiness', because 'this is good, and pleases

God our Saviour'.[24] This may be effected by deterring people from evil and lawlessness by means of either the threat or the imposition of suitable punishments; and it is specifically in this context that we are told that 'the law is made not for good men but for law-breakers and rebels, the ungodly and sinful, the unholy and irreligious; for those who kill their fathers or mothers, for murderers, for adulterers and perverts, for slave-traders and liars and perjurers', etc.[25]

*(c) The scope of the law*
In the Old Testament there are many cases of specific penalties being prescribed for particular offences, as in other codes of law in the ancient Near East; but a new state of affairs in this respect was foretold when Jesus said to the Jewish leaders: 'Therefore I tell you that the kingdom of God will be taken away from you and given to a people who will produce its fruit.'[26] It is perfectly true that, earlier in the same Gospel, it is recorded that he declared that he had 'not come to abolish the Law or the Prophets . . . but to fulfil them', and that he went on to say; 'I tell you the truth, until heaven and earth disappear, not the smallest letter, not the least stroke of a pen, will by any means disappear from the Law until everything is accomplished.'[27] But this does not mean that the whole legal system of the Old Testament is still in force.

For at this point we must make a necessary distinction – however little this would have been understood in Israel of old – between, first, the *moral* law, which Jesus perfectly fulfilled by his personal obedience to its every precept, by the vicarious death in which he took upon himself the curse pronounced on those who fail to do this,[28] and by re-imposing its standards on his followers – not as a means of salvation (which God had never intended it to be), but as a pattern of life; secondly, the *ceremonial* law, which was largely designed as a way of grace – although expressed, of course, in a legal form – and which had completely fulfilled its purpose (except by way of teaching) when Christ replaced its shadows and types by the substance of that supreme sacrifice to which all the animal sacrifices of the old covenant had pointed forward; and, thirdly, the *civil* and *criminal* law, which had been promulgated for the daily government of God's ancient, but very wayward, people and had served its purpose when the ethnic nation of Israel had been replaced by a redeemed community[29] drawn from 'every nation, tribe, people and language'[30] – all of whom are subject to God's moral law, but whose members must live, for the rest, under the civil and criminal legislation of the particular states to which they owe allegiance.

It is, therefore, the duty of each nation or group of nations to decide – according to a number of criteria which need not detain us now – which sins against God's moral law could, or should, be treated as crimes, and what other provisions (in themselves, it may be, of no moral significance) should be declared as offences against the State and punished accordingly. All this is a matter for debate and moral decision in a democracy, in which Christians should play their full part.

### (d) Forms of punishment

Nor, as I see it, are there any specific instructions in the Bible about what forms of punishment should be prescribed today; so this is another matter in which general moral principles should be applied. Any form of punishment which is degrading to those who either suffer or inflict it – as alike made 'in the image and likeness of God' – should, I feel sure, be repudiated; and torture or wanton cruelty are, as such, always degrading. (For a brief discussion of punishment under Islamic law see Additional Note.)

It may be helpful, at this point, to digress from our general argument to discuss a specific point of topical interest which may serve as a useful, if controversial, illustration: namely, the question whether capital punishment should be re-introduced in this country as the prescribed – or, alternatively, as a permissible – form of punishment for deliberate murder. The popular debate on this subject normally turns on whether the death penalty is, or is not, a uniquely effective deterrent; and this, in itself, is a matter of considerable controversy. Some people base their argument on statistics; but these would prove convincing only if it were possible to compare two wholly similar areas, in one of which the death penalty is in fact imposed in cases in which some other penalty had been substituted in the other; or, alternatively, if one could compare the statistics, over a sufficient number of years, where the death penalty had been applied, discarded, and then re-introduced in the same country. This is a matter of considerable difficulty; but it may, I think, confidently be stated that no convincing evidence has yet been produced either way.

Other people despise statistics in this context and assert,

instead, that it is a mere matter of common sense that the death penalty is a unique deterrent. But is it? At the moment when a condemned man is standing before the gallows it may well be true that most people would choose life imprisonment rather than death. But it is far from certain whether this consideration would have the same effect on many a murderer at the time when he committed his crime. Statistics show that, in the past, only a distinct minority of murderers have in fact been convicted, and about half of those on whom death sentences were passed were subsequently reprieved. They also show that most murderers are scarcely those who would have been likely to be deterred by the threat of the gallows. A fairly obvious exception to this might well be the professional thief who would, in any case, expect a long prison sentence for some major robbery, and might reason that to use a gun (in order to avoid arrest, or silence for ever a possible witness) would make little difference, under the present law, to his time of incarceration. But against this must be reckoned those eccentrics who long to call attention to themselves and might anticipate a ghoulish enjoyment in the excitement of a dramatic trial. In any case, the fact remains that the *Report of the Royal Commission on Capital Punishment*, 1953,[31] came to the considered conclusion that the quest for a satisfactory definition of different degrees of murder was 'chimerical' and should be abandoned.[32]

There are also, of course, some who would campaign against the death penalty in all cases, however effective it might be as a deterrent, on purely moral grounds. It seems to me, however, that no one who takes the Bible seriously as his final criterion can sustain the argument that this penalty is *never* permissible. Equally, there are others who hold that the Bible makes capital punishment *mandatory* in cases of deliberate murder. But with such an assertion I do not myself agree. It certainly cannot be based on the Mosaic legislation – both for reasons which I have already outlined and because it was there applied much more widely (and in circumstances in which few, if any, Christians would advocate it today). So those people who regard 'a life for a life' as mandatory commonly fall back on Genesis 9:5 and 6, which they regard as a sort of 'creation ordinance'. For myself, however, I cannot go along with this argument – for a number of reasons. First, the primary purpose of this passage seems to be to emphasize the unique value of human life in comparison with that of animals. Secondly, no distinction whatever is here made between murder and manslaughter – such as was covered later by the provisions regarding 'cities of refuge'.[33] Thirdly, this passage seems to be a sort of prelude to the *lex talionis* (i.e. the concept of an eye for an eye), as can be seen from the fact that it demands the death of an animal which may have caused a man's death.[34] To me, therefore, this passage is one of those that make the death penalty *permissible*, but not *mandatory*.[35]

So I believe that this question must, as I have already said, be decided on general moral grounds. In favour of the death penalty can be urged the retributive argument that this is the only punishment which adequately expresses the heinousness of the 'worst of crimes'. But while this is certainly the right description of some murders, it seems scarcely applicable, on purely moral grounds, to others. Another argument is the mental and moral breakdown which may well result from a very long prison sentence, especially when this has to be extended, in the interests of public safety, into really advanced years. Yet on the other side of the scales must be put the extreme difficulty in finding any satisfactory classification of different forms of murder; the distinct danger of an occasional miscarriage of justice; the fact that the execution of a terrorist might well turn him into a martyr; the anomaly of nursing an ill prisoner back to health just in order that he may then be put to death judicially; the horror of a long period of suspense and anticipation; and the trauma – for criminal, executioner and others – of the final act.

In conjunction with this review of the arguments concerning the death penalty, we should, perhaps, consider some of the corporal punishments prescribed in ancient Israel and other nations of antiquity, and in this country until not very long ago. Would such forms of punishment be right today? On the one side it may be said that they might prove a powerful deterrent, that they would help to ease the problem of our overcrowded prisons, and that they would transgress the bounds of just retribution only if they were excessively severe. On the other side it will have been noted that I have consistently sought to exclude any penalties which are 'cruel' or 'degrading' to the dignity of man made in the image of God.

So the question inevitably arises as to whether this standard of what is cruel or degrading is static or subject to change, and whether what was divinely permitted in the past may be inappropriate today. I myself would unhesitatingly answer this last question in the affirmative. Today we have witnessed, and become parties to, a whole series of Declarations, Conventions and Covenants about 'Human Rights' (themselves, as I have argued elsewhere, the largely unacknowledged offspring of the classical doctrine of 'Natural Law').[36] But should we, as Christians, go along with the more humane notions which are today internationally recognized (if all too seldom observed in practice) or should we ignore them – on the grounds that they are humanistic rather than biblical?

Let me make my own position clear. I believe that the Bible is our abiding authority in both doctrine and ethics, and that we have no right to abandon or transgress its principles. But I do not believe (as I have already said) that the *penalties* for crime, etc., in the Mosaic Law are in any sense binding on us today – as, in my view, the New Testament bears ample testimony. What, then, about an abstract standard such as what is, or is not, 'degrading' to mankind made in the image of God? Can that change? Again, I would say 'Yes'. Basic moral principles retain their abiding validity, but they will be differently interpreted and applied in various countries and successive ages. Modesty, for example, will always remain a Christian virtue; but no one can deny that what is considered to be modest or immodest in one age may, by general consent, be considered differently in another. And exactly the same, in my view, applies to those penalties which are now considered to be 'cruel and inhuman' – or, alternatively, degrading to human beings made in God's image.

### The role of the courts: practical problems

It is time now to return to my main thesis. The Bible, as it seems to me, makes it permissible for the State to take whatever steps appear to be necessary in order to maintain law and order, and to deter criminal behaviour, provided always that it does not have recourse to any measures which are unjust, cruel, degrading or arbitrary. Injustice is *never* permissible; the weak *must* be protected; and *no* man should be punished more severely than he deserves (for it must be remembered that even the old *lex talionis* represented the maximum, rather than any mandatory, requital). The obligation of the State to do all it can to *reform* criminals may, I think, be taken for granted; and in the present condition of our prisons, at least, this means that incarceration should be avoided in every case in which a viable alternative is available. Whenever feasible, offenders should be made to compensate their victims, or to repay the State such compensation as has already been awarded. Compulsory schemes of work for community welfare, and senior attendance centres at which football hooligans, for example, can be required to report at week-ends, should be encouraged; and funds must somehow be found for these and other imaginative experiments – for the prevention of crime is not a matter on which we can afford to be niggardly. It must also be remembered that the strongest deterrent is the likelihood of detection, so recruitment of suitable personnel for the police is a top priority.

*(a) The adversary system in criminal trials*
In the prevention and detection of crime, however, it is exceedingly difficult to strike the right balance between providing adequate safeguards against police corruption, on the one hand, and imposing excessive restrictions on their ability to protect society, on the other (see further Sir David McNee's discussion in Chapter III, pp. 76–80). In this context it might well be advisable to restrict the 'right to silence' at a trial (or, rather, the inferences which may legitimately be drawn from its exercise) in exchange for the elimination, or much tighter regulation, of police 'verbals'. In any case, I am not myself convinced that our much vaunted 'adversary procedure' in criminal courts is always superior to a more 'inquisitorial' form of trial. Ludovic Kennedy has gone so far as to write:

> Let no one pretend that our system of justice is a search for truth. It is nothing of the kind. It is a contest between two sides played according to certain rules, and if the truth happens to emerge as the result of the contest, then that is pure windfall . . . It is not something with which the contestants are concerned. They are concerned only that the game should be played according to the rules. There are many rules and one of them is that some questions which might provide a short cut to the truth are not allowed to be asked, and those that are asked are not allowed to be answered. The result is that verdicts are often reached haphazardly, for the wrong reasons, in spite of the evidence, and may or may not coincide with the literal truth. The tragedy of our courts is that means

have come to count more than ends, form more than content, appearance more than reality.[37]

Now this is certainly a caricature of the 'adversary system' – but, as in any clever caricature, the features it distorts are nonetheless recognizable. But what I should hate to see would be any curtailment of a genuinely judicial procedure, with forensic pleading and cross-examination in open court, in favour of the recommendations of some board of psychiatrists – or the abandonment of the verdict of a jury and the sentence of a judge in favour of the decision of some committee of faceless bureaucrats.

### (b) Sentencing by experts

It is precisely this point which gives me pause in regard to sentencing by 'experts'. It can, of course, plausibly be argued that the trial judge (with or without a jury) is ideally placed to decide whether the prisoner in the dock did, or did not, do what he is alleged to have done. He deals with this as a strict matter of fact on the basis of all the evidence. It is for this that he has been trained, and he usually does it more efficiently than anyone else is likely to do it. But when it comes to the question of sentence a very different problem arises. A judge commonly knows little about prison conditions, and certainly has no opportunity to see how well – or how badly – an individual offender will respond to these conditions. Would it not be wiser, then, to confine the duties of the judge to the single issue of 'guilty' or 'not guilty', and to leave it to 'experts' to decide the quite different question of what is to be done with the offender? Would not psychiatrists, for example, be much better placed than a judge to decide whether the individual concerned should be sent to a hospital or a prison, and for how long?

This would make excellent sense if the *only* purpose of criminal sanctions was the reform – or cure – of the offender. But there is clearly another side to the matter. In place of a public trial in open court, with suitable medical or psychiatric evidence which can always be challenged, such a system would mean that the fate of a man or woman judged 'guilty' at the original trial is left to a committee or series of committees, which would presumably sit – in general – behind closed doors, and which would come to their decision as a result of a number of factors, some of which might be of an exceedingly individual and subjective character, and none of which would be open to the cut and thrust of forensic argument. It may well be that these committees would do their work – in the main – exceedingly well, and that the result would in some respects represent an advance upon our present system. But I confess that I have my doubts. Such a system might conceivably aid the ideal of reform; but would it, or would it not, promote the cause of justice? Might it not give the offender the impression that he is being treated exclusively as a patient who has been made subject to a course of compulsory treatment of indeterminate length, rather than as a morally responsible human being who is being punished according to what were at least believed to be his deserts?

*(c) Justice and the different objectives of sentences*
Until quite recently, judges and even magistrates were left to find their own way through the maze of problems presented by the quest for the right sentence (in terms of both the crime and the criminal) with little or no training, guidance or preparation. A good deal is now being done to remedy this situation, and considerable progress has been made. But some of the problems posed are almost insoluble. It is clearly desirable, for example, that similar crimes should be similarly punished, wherever they are committed and whoever may try them, in order that justice may be *seen* to be done; but the fact remains that the precise circumstances of two apparently identical cases may in reality differ widely. Obviously enough, moreover, a fine – or, alternatively, a short prison sentence – which one man may take in his stride may mean ruin for another (and this applies, in part, even to the publicity which surrounds a trial). Again, the deterrent value of a heavy sentence for a crime which is becoming all too common is readily apparent; but there is a distinct danger that this may represent a palpable injustice in terms of some individual offender. By contrast, not only the protection of society but the considerations of abstract justice may well justify what would otherwise be an excessive sentence for a relatively minor offence in the case of one who has made a nuisance of himself in this way repeatedly.

It is precisely at this point that the complexity inherent in the question of the *purpose* of criminal sanctions becomes most acute. Statute law normally prescribes the *maximum* sentence for a specific crime,[38] but leaves the problem of how to grade a particular offence of that type to the discretion of the court concerned, which must frequently ask itself, in the words of Baroness Wootton (an influential thinker and writer on English penal policy), whether it is 'trying to administer justice, or aiming at reducing criminality'.[39] As I emphasized in my 1978 Hamlyn Lectures, Professor John Rawls of Harvard University insists that 'justice is the first virtue of social institutions, as truth is of systems of thought . . . Each person possesses an inviolability founded on justice that even the welfare of a society cannot override.'[40] But, after quoting these same words, Barbara Wootton comments; 'That is to say, we must never be unjust to one man in order to benefit others. That "to be just" means "to be fair" is probably an accepted linguistic usage, but the principle that justice must always override all other considerations is . . . an autonomous moral judgment which may or may not be acceptable to others.'[41]

Most courts, she says, adopt a sort of 'tariff' of sentences – reaching up only in the very worst cases to the prescribed maximum – graded according to the gravity of the particular circumstances. But this concept of gravity is itself somewhat nebulous, since 'the gravity of an offence may be judged either by its results,[42] or by assessments of the wickedness of the perpetrator's intentions.'[43] But, whichever criterion is adopted, sentencing on this basis 'is both historically and logically linked with the moralistic principle of making the punishment fit the crime' and, as such, relates to past events; whereas

> what has come to be known as the reductivist sentence looks to the future, in that it gives priority to the objective of diminishing the prospect of future criminality. Sometimes this leads to greater leniency than the tariff would suggest; sometimes, on the other hand, to greater severity and to a disregard of Rawls's principle of the individual's right of justice.[44]

This represents a particularly good example of the fact that the administration of criminal justice imposes on the courts the obligation to attempt the virtually impossible feat of striking a balance between at least two conflicting principles. My own view – for what it may be worth – is that the 'moralistic principle' of equal justice must always be regarded as *basic*, but that the courts must be free to modify this in favour of leniency where they feel that this would be likely to be of genuine benefit to the individual concerned without having a disproportionately unfortunate effect on other offenders, potential offenders, or the community at large. I am much more doubtful about cases of excessive severity – although I recognize, of course, that leniency to one person must, in itself, make the sentences imposed on others appear, in some degree at least, to be unfair.

**Conclusion**
It is clearly impossible, on the human level, to make the different aims of criminal punishment, as I have tried to define them, fit into a wholly coherent system. This is reflected in the interplay of what Barbara Wootton terms the 'reductivist' and the 'moralistic' principles in sentencing, which can be seen in the historical development of sentencing powers in this country from the turn of the present century. It is only since 1907 that convicted persons have been permitted to appeal against their sentences, and the courts were given new powers to deal with the offender as an individual, rather than follow the 'punitive' or tariff approach implicit in the legislation of previous centuries. It was in 1907, too, that the Probation of Offenders Act heralded this 'individualization' of sentences which has, over the years, been greatly extended and now includes suspended prison sentences, community service orders, etc.

As. D. A. Thomas, a leading authority on English criminal law and sentencing, puts it:

> The effect of this legislative structure is to create two distinct systems of sentencing, reflecting different penal objectives and governed by different principles. The sentencer is presented with a choice: he may impose, usually in the name of general deterrence, a sentence intended to reflect the offender's culpability, or he may seek to influence his future behaviour by subjecting him to an appropriate measure of supervision, treatment, or protective confinement . . . Achievement of the broader objectives of a punitive sentence may require the sentencer to adopt an approach which is not likely to

assist the offender towards conformity with the law in future, and indeed may positively damage such prospects of future conformity as exist already, while a measure designed to assist the offender to regulate his behaviour in the future may appear to diminish the gravity of the offence and weaken the deterrent effect of the law on potential offenders.[45]

The position is, indeed, further complicated by a number of other factors. The tariff system itself, for example, 'represents a complex of penal theories', as we have already seen. But here 'the overriding principle of proportionality between offence and sentence applies whatever motivating theory supports the sentence.'[46] By contrast, 'cases in which the primary decision is likely to be in favour of an individualised measure can be identified by the characteristics of the offender' – particularly in regard to 'young offenders', 'offenders in need of psychiatric treatment', 'recidivists who appear to have reached a critical point in their life' and 'persistent recidivists who are in danger of becoming completely institutionalized as a result of repeated sentences of imprisonment'.[47]

It is of axiomatic importance that, as far as possible, justice should always be seen to be done. So I must repeat what I have already said in passing: namely, that a just proportion between crime and penalty should always be regarded as the *basic norm*; and that, when this norm is abandoned (as I believe it often should be) in favour of a more lenient sentence which may either prevent the offender from starting on a life of crime, or halt his downward path, or represent a recognition of his particular need for some remedial treatment, then this should be made clear in the judgment – so that it does not come to be regarded as a mere matter of course. Most people share (in some degree, at least) what I believe is a God-given craving for justice and a sense of outrage when this is compromised or denied. So it is very important to do our best to recognize this and to explain precisely what course of action is being taken, and why.[48] But only God himself (as we have seen) is perfectly just, for he alone knows all the facts, understands his creatures through and through, and can reconcile the irreconcilable. Human justice, at its best, can never be more than a very imperfect and faltering imitation of his. Yet this, and nothing less, *must* be our aim; and, if we do all we can to achieve this, then we can rest back on the conviction that there remains a final Assize at which everything now hidden will be revealed, and everything now wrong will *somehow* be set right.

## Additional note on punishment under Islamic Law

In view of the widespread interest I encounter today in regard to the threatened (or actual) re-introduction, in a number of Muslim countries, of some of the savage punishments pre-scribed under the classical Islamic law for a few precisely defined offences, a further reference to this subject may be relevant. The offences concerned include 'apostasy' from Islam, for which a Muslim was always subject to the death penalty. This would now, of course, constitute a grave breach of the Universal Declaration of Human Rights; and some modern Muslims argue that it was originally prescribed when Islam was still on the defensive, and apostasy was tantamount to treachery. In any case, this penalty would today be invoked only in Saʻudi Arabia, I think – although extremist groups of Muslims have been demanding its re-introduction in Egypt, Iran and elsewhere. For illicit sex relations the prescribed punishment is stoning, in the case of anyone who has ever enjoyed a valid marriage, and a hundred lashes for one who has not. Both penalties[49] would be applied in Saʻudi Arabia, and the lashes (but not stoning) have been re-introduced in Libya, Pakistan and Iran.[50] Theft is punishable by the amputation of the right hand, and brigandage by that of the right hand and left foot – or even by impalement, if anyone has been killed. These penalties, too, are applicable today in Saʻudi Arabia, while the penalty for theft has been re-imposed in Libya, and at least discussed elsewhere. For slander of a 'chaste' Muslim's chastity, or for the consumption by a Muslim of even the smallest amount of alcohol (except under doctor's orders, or in cases of extreme necessity) lashes, again, are prescribed. But the fact remains that under the classical Islamic law most of these penalties could *very* seldom be lawfully applied because of the almost impossible standard of proof demanded. As for murder, manslaughter and wounding, these were treated, for the most part, as civil wrongs rather than crimes, and it was left to the 'heirs of blood' to demand either talion or 'blood-money', or even to pardon the aggressor, in suitable cases. For the rest, the punishment for any wrong-doing was left to the discretion of the courts, although almost all recognized authorities insist that the most severe 'discretionary' punishment must not exceed the lightest prescribed penalty.[51] But this rule is largely ignored in Sa'udi Arabia, for example, where grossly excessive punishments are often inflicted and offenders have been known to die under the lash.[52] Few people today, even in Muslim countries, are happy about such punishments.

# Notes and References

1 Formerly Professor of Jurisprudence in the University of Oxford and subsequently Principal of Brasenose College.
2 Cf. *Punishment and Responsibility: Essays in the Philosophy of Law* (O.U.P., 2nd printing, 1969), p.1.
3 Ibid., p. 3.
4 Ibid., p. 79 (footnote).
5 Ibid., pp. 79 f.
6 For a critique of this view, see C. S. Lewis, *Undeceptions* (Geoffrey Bles, London, 1971), pp. 238 f. and Hart, op. cit., pp. 81 f.
7 I have ignored in this context those 'crimes' which consist in nothing more than the infringement of some statutory regulation and which involve no moral obloquy *per se*.
8 Incidentally, I think William Temple was distinctly sanguine when, in his Clarke Hall Lecture 'The Ethics of Penal Action', 1934, he classified the effect on the offender himself of all such measures as 'reformative'. They may, in fact, be 'reformative', 'deterrent', or both.
9 'Danger' can be taken to include the possibility of the offender being responsible, in the future, for offences involving serious physical injury, serious psychological effects which impair a person's enjoyment of life (for example, some sexual offences), exceptional personal hardship (for example, financial loss which markedly affects a person's way of life), or damage to the security of the state (for example, as a result of espionage), or to the general fabric of society. These elements of 'dangerousness' have been identified by the Advisory Council on the Penal System in their report *Sentences of Imprisonment* (HMSO, London, 1978), p. 89.
10 1 John 4:8 and 16.
11 1 John 1:5.
12 Joel 2:25.
13 2 Samuel 12:13 and Psalm 51.
14 Cf. Proverbs 3:11 and 12.
15 Hebrews 12:10 f.
16 Cf. 2 Thessalonians 1:9.
17 Cf. Matthew 5:22, 29 f.; 10:28; 18:9; 23:33; etc.
18 Hebrews 4:13.
19 Hebrews 4:12.
20 Psalm 119:75.
21 Romans 13:1.

22  1 Peter 2:14.
23  Romans 13:3 ff.
24  1 Timothy 2:2 f.
25  1 Timothy 1:9 f.
26  Matthew 21:43.
27  Matthew 5:17 f.
28  Galatians 3:10 and 13.
29  1 Peter 2:9.
30  Revelation 7:9.
31  Cmd. 8932.
32  Cf. Hart op. cit., p. 60, etc. Cf. also Barbara Wootton, *Crime and Penal Policy* (Allen and Unwin, London, 1978), pp. 137 ff.
33  Numbers 35:11.
34  As in several primitive codes of law.
35  For a fuller discussion, see my *Issues of Life and Death* (Hodder & Stoughton, 1976), pp. 108–112.
36  Cf. *Liberty, Law and Justice* (Stevens, London, 1978), pp. 15 ff.
37  *The Trial of Stephen Ward* (Gollancz, 1964), p. 251 – quoted in Wootton, op. cit., pp.19 f.
38  But the Report of the Advisory Council on the Penal System (*Sentences of Imprisonment*, HMSO, 1978) has recently suggested that these maximum penalties (most of which are scarcely ever imposed in practice) should be replaced by those maxima which are commonly accepted as such by the courts, but that special provision should be made for that ten per cent (perhaps) of 'exceptional offenders' who pose real danger to the public (cf. n.9 above), in regard to whom no express maximum sentence in terms of years should be prescribed. This proposal would, *inter alia*, abolish the present mandatory sentence of life imprisonment for murder, and would instead allow a court to pass either a specified or an indeterminate sentence, and also to make suitable non-custodial provision for cases of 'diminished responsibility', 'mercy killing', etc.
39  *Crime and Penal Policy* (Allen and Unwin, London, 1978), pp. 34, etc.
40  *Liberty, Law and Justice* (Stevens, London, 1978), p. 35.
41  Op. cit., p. 35.
42  E.g. what injury or loss the victim in fact suffers.
43  Op. cit., p. 36.
44  Op. cit., p. 37.
45  *Principles of Sentencing* (2nd ed., Heinemann, London, 1979), p. 8.
46  Ibid., p. 14.
47  Ibid., p. 17.
48  E.g. What sort of sentence the offence merited, and why this was being mitigated, or even suspended or remitted altogether, in this particular case.
49  Except that the normal form of execution in Sa'udi Arabia is now in all cases decapitation.
50  In Iran some persons accused of grave sexual offences have, moreover, recently been executed by a firing squad.
51  Although there is an occasional reference to 'exceptional circumstances'.

52 I should add that many of the trials and sentences reported from Iran since the revolution have little or no semblance of legality. They represent a harsh reaction against the abuses of law perpetrated under the Shah.

# III Policing Modern Britain

Sir David McNee

## Introduction

The task assigned to me is to discuss how the police service operates within our criminal justice system. So let me relate my talk on modern policing to how I see this important responsibility, first as a man wholly devoted to the service of Jesus Christ (though I know that I have many failures in fulfilling that service), and secondly as the man who as Commissioner of Police of the Metropolis at present holds a unique place in the British Police Service.[1]

In case you may think I was born with a silver spoon in my mouth, perhaps I should briefly tell you something of my background. Glasgow was my birthplace, and I was brought up in that (to use the words of St Paul) 'no mean city' during the years of the depression. This was the formative period of my life. Had it not been for the influence of the evangelical church to which I belonged and of my godly parents, I doubt if I would be addressing you now.

It was in that same great city that I began my career as a police officer, walking the same streets that I had known as a boy. Later I was to serve there for many years as a detective. I learned at first hand about urban deprivation and crime. The knowledge I gained then about the needs of the public and the ways of the criminal remained with me as Deputy Chief Constable in the county of Dunbarton, Chief of Glasgow and Strathclyde, and now finally as Commissioner.

## The roles of the police – past and present

Some people have a view of police which sees us very much as a force: oppressors of the public. Nothing could be further from the truth. We are primarily a service. That is our strength, and it allows us to apply force only when it becomes necessary as the last resort. This has been borne out by research, which shows that the majority of police work is about helping people and not (if I dare use the phrase) about 'hammering' them. We have been described in one socio-logical review as the only twenty-four hour a day, seven days a week, fully mobile social service (and without the right to strike, at that).[2]

Compassion constrained by an understanding of human weakness: to the student of history that is one of the recurring themes throughout the development of modern British policing. Modern policing, as we know it in Britain, began on 29th September 1829 when the first constables of the newly formed Metropolitan Police stepped out of their station houses for the first time on to the streets of London. These men owed their existence to the acumen of the Home Secretary of the day, Sir Robert Peel.[3]

Peel by some political sleight of hand introduced a 'Bill for Improving the Police in and Near the Metropolis', and succeeded in having it passed by both Houses of Parliament without a vestige of serious opposition, although at that time there was a general feeling of abhorrence toward the whole concept of a police force in this country. If, however, the beginnings of the Metropolitan Police were the work of Peel, the building of the force was the work of the two men he appointed as joint Commissioners of the Force – Charles Rowan and Richard Mayne.

Police forces quickly reduced crime, which had mush-roomed in the industrial rush to urbanization. Disorder was brought under control, and the need for repression by military force was thereby removed, with a consequent reduction of casualties. By maintaining the peace, police gave people a new-found freedom and security, which generated mobility and allowed business and social intercourse to grow. At the same time, a police presence eliminated the need to carry arms. It was police who facilitated the conduct of local and national elections. They thus helped to make possible the expansion of the franchise in an age when force and intimidation at elections often called for a military presence and action.[4] As Charles Reith (one of the foremost of police historians) explains:

> The police ended quickly the appalling farce, injustice and corruption of prosecution and procedure in criminal cases in the courts. They ended the brutal forms of victimization by employers of innocent workers who

dared to advocate co-operative action in protest against their exploitation; and ended also the murders of employers and vitriol-throwing and other savage means by which some workers sought revenge. It was the existence of police and their ability to enforce laws and to secure a wide measure of legal justice that enabled the Trades Union and Labour movements in Britain to take root and grow and prosper.[5]

This success was largely due to the sound philosophy established and consistently reinforced by Rowan and Mayne. Principles first laid down by them as the foundations of policing[6] are still contained in three paragraphs of the Metropolitan Police Instruction Book which is issued to every officer when he joins the Force. These paragraphs have become a creed to be learned by heart. They read as follows:

The primary object of an efficient Police Force is the prevention of crime; the next that of detection and punishment of offenders if crime is committed. To those ends all the efforts of the Police must be directed. The protection of life and property, the preservation of public tranquillity, and the absence of crime, will alone prove whether those efforts have been successful, and whether the objects for which the police were appointed have been attained.

In attaining these objects, much depends on the approval and co-operation of the public, and these have always been determined by the degree of esteem and respect in which the police are held. Therefore every member of the Force must remember that it is his duty to protect and help members of the public, no less than to bring offenders to justice. Consequently, while prompt to prevent crime and arrest criminals, he must look on himself as the servant and guardian of the general public and treat all law-abiding citizens, irrespective of their race, colour, creed or social position, with unfailing patience and courtesy.

By the use of tact and good humour the public can normally be induced to comply with directions, and thus the necessity for using force, with its possible public disapproval, is avoided. He who in this way secures the object he has in view is a more useful police officer than his comrade who, relying too much on the assertion of his authority, runs the risk of seeing that authority challenged and possibly, for the time being, over-borne. If, however, persuasion, advice or warning is found to be ineffective, a resort to force may become necessary, as it is imperative that a police officer, being required to take action, shall act with the firmness necessary to render it effective.[7]

In the view of the members of the 1962 Royal Commission on the Police these instructions admirably summarize the requirements for a sound relationship between the police and the public.[8] The quality of this relationship has been examined in numerous public opinion polls and attitude surveys. The results of these have indicated the high regard that the British people generally have for their police. For example, one survey by Professor Belson of the London School of Economics showed that ninety percent of people or more liked, respected, trusted and were satisfied with the police.[9] This kind of regard always comes as a surprise to police officers who consistently expect people to think rather less of them than they actually do. It is unlikely, however, that this regard stems from the absence of crime and disorder by which it is suggested the efficiency of the police be measured.

**Crime today**
The merest glance at the official crime statistics (and for all the academic caveats they attract, the official statistics remain the most valid and reliable measure of criminal activity available) presents an horrific picture, with a fourfold increase in serious crime over the last twenty years. 1978 saw crime in London fall for the first time for eight years, a pattern repeated throughout the country as a whole. But with indictable crimes still exceeding the half million mark, a slight reduction in the crime figures provides little comfort.[10]
Of particular concern are the swingeing increases in offences where either violence against the person is explicit or there is an underlying element or a likelihood of violence. Since 1958 in London homicide has gone up by nearly one hundred and fifty percent, and over the same period rape has increased by almost four hundred percent. Woundings and assaults have gone from 1700 to more than 13,000 a year; burglaries from 20,000 a year to 122,000; and thefts from the

person from less than one thousand to more than 16,000 a year. Robbery has increased from just over 400 in 1958 to 6594 last year – a rise of more than 1500 percent.

A great deal of this crime is committed by young people. It is impossible to say exactly how much, but a third of all persons arrested in London for serious crime are juveniles – young people aged from ten to sixteen years of age. And more than half the arrests for serious crime are of people under the age of twenty-one.

I apologize for throwing that succession of figures at you. Statistics tend to have a soporific effect on many people. But I cannot think of a more emphatic way of highlighting the dramatic increase in crime that has taken place in recent years. As one sociological commentator has put it:

> A multitude could tell the same story as myself, of an urban area going rapidly downhill under a relentless wave of vandalism, arson and violence.[11]

The commentator in question was Patricia Morgan. She went on to say:

> Yet, we are frequently told, neither the statistics nor our observations of events are evidence of a 'real' increase in lawbreaking.[12]

She drew attention to research in Sheffield which suggested that

> The man in the street may not be wrong after all. This work and other studies, showing that victims' decisions to report offences are remarkably stable over factors such as time and socio-economic status, suggest that if people are seeing and reporting more crimes these days, it is probably due to the simple fact that there really are more to be seen and reported.[13]

She will perhaps be encouraged by the fact that policemen who observe criminal behaviour as a matter of their daily routine (unlike most academic researchers whose studies are limited in time, place and purpose) are in no doubt about the figures. Over recent years there has been a real and marked increase in crime, and crime by young people has increased particularly fast.

To say merely that crime has increased markedly is only half the story, however. For whilst it tells about the extent of the problem, it says nothing of its gravity. Statistical analysis of the crime figures continues to confirm the comments made in 1972 by Mr Stanley Klein, then principal crime statistician at the Home Office, that

> Over 95 per cent of crimes are offences against property. Offences of violence against the person fluctuate between 2 percent and 3 percent of the total; these and sexual offences are never more than 5 percent of all recorded crime.[14]

This repeating pattern, together with the facts that theft offences dominate the crime figures and that about seventy percent of the property reported stolen is under twenty-five pounds in value, leads some people to argue that most crime is 'trivial'. I suppose it really depends what is meant by trivial. But I suspect that few crimes are seen as trivial by their victims, many of whom are the more vulnerable members of our communities. The trauma that many people suffer as a result of criminal behaviour – despite its apparent triviality to the dispassionate academic eye – is not easily assessed. The fact of it, however, does much to undermine the argument that the majority of crime is of a trivial nature.[15]

**The Royal Commission on Criminal Procedure**
In this climate of rising crime the announcement in 1977 that there was to be a Royal Commission on Criminal Procedure which would examine, among other things, the powers and duties of police in the investigation of criminal offences and the rights and duties of suspects and accused persons, was received with mixed feelings. The opportunity of laying bare many of the difficulties which surround law enforcement and the investigation of crime was welcomed. There was, however, a general feeling within the service that the Commission had been established largely in consequence of one exceptional case – the death of Maxwell Confait – for the purpose of placing yet further restrictions on the police.[16]

The point has been made by two eminent criminologists, Sir Leon Radzinowicz and Joan King: 'A society which would wholly repress crime would, in the process, have to repress all initiative, all non-conformity, all adaptation to change. There

Commission in terms of improving safeguards for individuals accused of criminal offences. It is interesting to note that when the Prime Minister announced on the 23rd June 1977 that a Royal Commission was to be set up, he made it plain that there were other considerations. 'In recent years,' he said, 'there have been a number of reforms adopted or proposed with the object of improving the safeguards for individuals accused of criminal offences. The pressure for changes in this direction continues. On the other hand there has been a continuing rise in the level of crime, and it is increasingly being argued that the job of the police in fighting crime and in seeing that offenders (and particularly dangerous professional criminals) are brought to justice, is being made unwarrantably difficult by the restraints of criminal procedure. There is a balance to be struck here between the interest of the whole community and the rights and liberties of the individual citizen. The Government consider that the time has come for the whole criminal process from investigation to trial to be reviewed with that fundamental balance in mind. This will be the central task of this Royal Commission.'

In attacking the police evidence to the Royal Commission the National Council for Civil Liberties has argued that the police have lost sight of the need to safeguard the innocent and of the need to win and retain the co-operation of the public. The first of these two charges is not borne out by the facts, since if the evidence of the Metropolitan Police is read as a whole it can be seen that it seeks to safeguard and clarify the rights of the individual who is innocent until proven guilty.

As to the second charge, no police officer is going to jeopardize the very special relationship that exists between the British people generally and their police. The police proposals are unlikely to have any such effect. In fact, it was concern about that relationship which prompted police evidence to the Royal Commission. Decent people have nothing to fear from the police proposals: they have much to gain, for the proposals are aimed at improving police effectiveness and at preserving freedom for everybody, so that they may live peacefully in the security of their homes and go about the streets of London and our other towns and cities without fear.

Rejection of these charges put forward by the National Council for Civil Liberties must not be taken as a rejection of the Council and its members. Frequent as our disagreements may be, in a democracy law and order is a central issue and is rightly a matter for constant debate. Irritating as police may find them from time to time, organizations such as the NCCL are an invaluable part of the complex machinery of checks and balances within our democratic society. They provide a channel for the voice of those who are genuinely nervous of police power and authority.

**Arresting 'suspected persons'**
There is a growing tendency in the ongoing debate about policing, of which the Royal Commission is but a part, for people to confuse (sometimes deliberately I think) the use of police powers with their abuse. Nowhere is that better seen than in the current campaign for the repeal of Section 4 of the Vagrancy Act, 1824, which gives the police certain powers to arrest persons they suspect are intending to commit a crime. Those involved in what has become known as the 'Anti-Sus Campaign' have concentrated on the fact that in London in particular a high proportion of arrests under Section 4 are of young black people. Typically, a report or paper is produced listing a number of cases which purport to be examples of how police officers abuse or misuse, deliberately or mistakenly, their powers under Section 4. (These 'cases' are rarely identifiable and give only the defendant's version of events.) With this as evidence (if that is what it can be called), it is then alleged that Section 4 is having a detrimental effect upon relations between black communities and the police. Therefore, the argument proceeds, in the interests of racial harmony Section 4 of the Vagrancy Act should be repealed.

An unjustifiable step has been taken in the argument. Beginning with specific, albeit selectively vague examples, it concludes that because of these alleged abuses police should lose the general use of a power which there is no objective evidence to suggest operates other than perfectly satisfactorily in the main.

An important point that people miss is that Section 4 does not give police the power to arrest anyone they feel suspicious about. There has to be a pattern of behaviour (and more than one suspicious act) which makes it clear to the officer and the court that the intention of the person was to commit a crime if a suitable opportunity arose. There are many situations where the criminal intent of a person is plain to see, but where no other offence has been committed nor an attempt been constituted.

It would be intolerable if criminals were to be allowed to loiter in the streets selecting their victims or targets free from police interference. Society has the right to be protected in such circumstances. It is the classic dilemma of law and order, balancing the need to safeguard people from criminals with the need to protect a person's right to behave as he or she thinks fit.

That police officers can be mistaken and that some may misuse the powers and authority of their office is undeniable. That is so in respect of every power they have, but it is no reason to take that power away from all. The only need is for the person concerned to be dealt with for that abuse – and dealt with firmly.

I know that some members of the black community are genuinely concerned about this law. Whether their concern is the result of police action or the consequence of political rhetoric is another matter. Certainly the campaign has not helped the cause of race relations. For however sincere they may be, by creating an atmosphere in which myth and rumour flourish and by providing a fertile field for the growth of distorted and harmful stereotypes, the campaigners have increased the difficulties faced by police officers in their attempts to establish good relations with black youth.

**The police and ethnic minorities**
The need to bridge the gap which exists in some places between the police on the one side and some sections of the black community and other ethnic minority groups on the other is crucial. Law and order in London and other large conurbations is now firmly linked to issues of race.

London has for a long time been the home of immigrants from many other countries who have settled and integrated within a few generations. The arrival, in large numbers, of people distinguished from the indigenous community by the colour of their skin has run rather less smoothly than earlier settlements. Black is beautiful but the difference in colour has made discrimination easier and heightened its insidious effects. A new dimension has been added to policing.

Since the early fifties many people from the New Commonwealth have come to London, settled and raised their families. Today it is estimated that they and their children (and in some cases their children's children) number about ten percent of London's population; and seventy percent of

them live in the deprived Inner City.[20] Poverty and deprivation bear heavily upon ethnic minorities and fuel the fires of
racial tension and conflict. Parallels have been drawn between
the situation in London now and that which existed in the
major cities of the United States at the time of the race riots in
the 1960s.

The black community is also a young community; and
youth and deprivation are bound up with the commission of
crime. Chuck Colson has already discussed (in Chapter I) the
determinist view that delinquency is a response to deprivation. To suggest that deprivation is a justification for crime is
to deny man's freedom of choice and to insult millions of
people who are poor, deprived and honest. I agree with him
that there is autonomy and choice in human affairs, and that
delinquency is not a blind or helpless response to deprivation,
despite the fact that it has become intellectually fashionable in
some quarters to regard it so. Nevertheless, the connections
between crime, youth and deprivation bring police officers
into open conflict with black youngsters committing crime.
Mutual animosity, suspicion and distrust grow. Myths develop about police harassment on the one side and black
criminality on the other, and become accepted as fact.

Peter Evans, Home Affairs correspondent of *The Times*,
discusses the problem in his book *The Police Revolution*:

> The most persistent and vociferous critics of the police
> are black people. No point of friction is potentially more
> dangerous than with young blacks. The irony is that the
> reaction of some police and immigrant groups is remark-
> ably similar. When friction does occur, each side tends to
> stand on its dignity, close ranks and think in stereotypes
> about the other, expecting the worst of it.[22]

With a tradition of policing that relies heavily for its effectiveness on public support and goodwill, the task of policing West
Indian and Asian communities (the young Asian is barely less
critical than the young black) is both difficult and volatile.

It is of course fertile ground for extremists who seek to
make political capital out of racial issues. Whether from the
left or the right of the political spectrum, the extremists feed
off each other and keep London's multi-racial melting pot at
boiling point. Solutions to the racial tension, which is fast
becoming an integral part of inner city life, are vital to the

future wellbeing of everybody – black, brown, white, West Indian, Asian, English or Scot.

The Parliamentary Select Committee on Race Relations and Immigration observed in 1977, in their investigation into the problems of the West Indian community, that the main bones of contention were discrimination, educational under-achievement and a feeling of alienation among young black people, but they said:

> Overriding them is the problem of environmental depri-
> vation, with all it connotes in terms of housing, employ-
> ment and social conditions, and which is fundamental
> and basic to most of the grievances felt by the West
> Indian communities.[23]

In a meeting I had last year with leaders of the Bangladeshi community in the East End, these were also the issues that concerned them and which they were looking to me to deal with. I am not one to shirk responsibility, but these are questions of social justice and a matter for local and national government. Their solution does not lie within the remit of police, although it is police officers who in the main have to face up to the consequences of them.

Because we are in the front line, the police service becomes associated in the minds of the minorities with all their frustra-tions and grievances against authority. The consequent danger is that the service may become isolated from the communities it has to police. The need to establish good relations with minorities is a main priority for police. A concerted attack is being made on the myths and misunder-standings in several ways: by police officers going into schools, by initiating and becoming involved in community projects and youth activities, by establishing close contacts and liaison with a variety of community leaders and organization; and also – and perhaps most important of all – by in-service train-ing.

Officers from my Community Relations Branch are in-creasingly involved in all Metropolitan Police training pro-grammes, from recruit training to pre-promotion courses. Their participation, together with the social studies content of the courses, helps to satisfy the need for introspection (the look in the mirror that all of us must take from time to time). It facilitates the educative process in which an awareness of community problems and needs is enhanced and the police role in meeting them is examined. The more traditional outward-looking approach to community relations, stimulating public support for law enforcement, falls largely upon Community Liaison Officers on districts. The activities of these officers within local communities are many and varied, but the basis of their effort is an extensive schools programme.

## The police and young people

Public support needs to be earned, and young people have to be encouraged to play their part. For this reason I have had our involvement with schools intensified over the past twelve months. Police officers going into schools, whether to talk about road safety, crime, the role of police, law and the courts, or the rights and duties of citizens, is long-term crime prevention. It provides an opportunity for police officers and local children to get to know one another.

How important this kind of contact is may best be illustrated by relating a story I told when giving the Basil Henriques Lecture at the annual meeting of the National Association of Boys' Clubs last year.[24] It was a story about a girl named Ann. That is not her real name, and when you have heard her story you will understand the reason for my discretion.

Ann's story began eighteen years ago when she was abandoned by her mother at birth. She was taken into care and subsequently adopted. When she was thirteen Ann made her first attempt to commit suicide by taking an overdose of aspirins whilst at school. A year later she ran away from home, but fortunately was found after a few days. In January of the following year she ran away again, and this time committed a burglary. She was then made the subject of a care order. But although the social worker took a great deal of interest in her, Ann's adoptive parents now rejected her.

Absconding from care became the pattern of her life. Six times Ann attempted suicide whilst in London, by taking an overdose of drugs. Almost inevitably she became involved in sexual offences with older men and contracted venereal disease. She committed further crimes of burglary, theft and taking and driving away. Ann was reported missing at least twelve times from six different remand homes, being found as far apart as Aberdeen and Brighton. Finally she was sent for borstal training, and three months later gave birth to a baby boy. Before her son was barely six months old, however, she took another overdose of drugs – her eighth – and died.

Ann's tragic story is a dramatic example of how our society is failing young people like her, as it fails the victims of their crimes. And the tragedy is that the story of Ann is not an isolated case. There are many more – far too many – such stories. Often during my career as a police officer I have seen similar cases of delinquency and desperation by young people who come from a broken home or from a family where parental guidance is minimal or non-existent.

A whole string of people failed Ann, including police. The identification of children at risk is a crucial responsibility of the police; and we are often better placed than other agencies to spot those who are most vulnerable. Metropolitan Police Juvenile Bureaux, which are headed by my Community Liaison Officers, have therefore been made into co-ordinating centres which involve police with care proceedings and cases of non-accidental injury to children. The arrangements have facilitated the development of close co-operation with other agencies. As mutual confidence and respect grow, hopefully the suspicion that exists about police involvement in this area will be overcome.

### The police and the responsible community

The aim of the police as always is to win and maintain the confidence of the people they serve. 'Public confidence is neither static nor homogeneous; it ebbs and flows, differing between communities and age groups, and it is sensitive to a wide variety of factors. Predominant is the ability of police to satisfy legitimate demands made on them.'[25]

One of these legitimate demands is that policemen have high moral standards and work within the law they are expected to uphold. Deliberate misuse of his office is the worst sin a police officer can commit; it is a complete betrayal of trust. It would be foolish to think that policing will ever be completely free of corruption and dishonesty. If people are to retain their confidence in the police, measures need to be taken to make corruption difficult to commit, to ensure that it is detected at an early stage when it does occur, and to apply incisive surgery before the malignancy begins to grow. Much has been said recently about police corruption. No one should be in any doubt that there is a great determination, not just by me but throughout the service, to pursue such crime ruthlessly and vigorously. This is happening now.

Throughout this discussion of the British policing tradition and of some of the current problems which are putting it to the test, the underlying theme has been the need to secure the confidence and co-operation of the public. Whatever the future holds for the police service, *that* must continue to be the overriding aim. For law and order in this country is a joint exercise between the people and the police. Therefore the bleak view of the future taken by Leslie Male when he was Chairman of the Police Federation in 1975 is not one I share. What he said was:

> We look into the future and see policemen being murdered; areas of the countryside where people are frightened to walk about; civil disorder on the in-crease . . .[26]

He went on to say '. . . and we want to draw everyone's attention to the situation in the hope that we can prevent it getting worse.'

In that sentence there is both an implied acknowledgement that responsibility for keeping law and order is in the hands of us all and also a tacit recognition that people can take action to turn things for the better.

Action is not always easy, however. Many people seem to have an aversion to getting involved in other people's personal crises – however desperate. This is a universal phenomenon that appears to be increasingly common to urban life.[27] Only the more lurid and salacious incidents hit the headlines; yet it is not uncommon to read newspaper stories such as that which appeared last December:

> A teenage girl was bundled into a taxi in front of hundreds of passers-by by two men who took her to a house and raped her.[28]

Even more shocking was a story in one of the national dailies a few weeks ago:

> The rape of a 54-year old spinster was watched in amusement by a crowd of Post Office workers . . . the men were on a platform at Waterloo Station when the

last train from Clapham pulled in – with the rape going on in one of the brightly lit carriages. They thought they were watching a free late-night sex show and eventually wandered away without calling for help.[29]

True, it is not always clear whether positive action on our part will be welcomed or not. But what is happening to our sense of social responsibility when a crowd of grown men can walk away from an obvious rape and do nothing? Is there no room for the Samaritan impulse in our cities today?

**A New Testament perspective**
St Paul was in no doubt about where our responsibilities lie. In his letter to the Romans he explains his understanding both of the Christian gospel and of its practical implications for the lives of Christians. In chapter 13 we find a discussion of our responsibilities, first towards the law and then towards one another.[30] In the words of the Living Bible (an American paraphrase):

3. For the magistrate does not frighten people who are doing right; but those doing evil will always fear him. So if you don't want to be afraid, keep the laws and you will get along well.
4. The magistrate is sent by God to help you. But if you are doing something wrong, of course you should be afraid, for he will have you punished. He is sent by God for that very purpose.
5. Obey the laws, then, for two reasons: first, to keep from being punished, and, second, just because you know you should.

Any system of authority is open to abuse by those who wield the power.[31] In talking about man's duty to the State, St Paul was making the point that where a just system prevails, the law should be used and observed. He goes on to apply the mortar to the bricks of Christian duty to authority when he discusses the Christian's responsibility to other people.

8. Pay all your debts, except the debt of love for others – never finish paying that! For if you love them, you will be obeying all of God's laws, fulfilling all his requirements.

9. If you love your neighbour as much as you love yourself you will not want to harm or cheat him, or kill him
   or steal from him. And you won't sin with his wife or
   want what is his, or do anything else the Ten
   Commandments say are wrong. All are wrapped up in
   this one, to love your neighbour as you love yourself.

This then is the core of a Christian's social responsibility –
love your neighbour as yourself.


**Conclusion**
Society is at one of history's crossroads. And if we want a God-
fearing, compassionate and caring world, then we all have
to work together to bring it about. There is an urgent need for
everyone to set high standards of behaviour – in our schools,
in our places of work, in our sports grounds and other public
places, in our dealings with each other, and above all in our
families.

Parental responsibility is crucial to the wellbeing of us all.
Personalities are not born – they are 'made' and developed in
the process of growing up; and the major influence comes
from one's parents. Standards and examples set by parents are
likely to remain with people throughout their life, until they in
turn pass them on to their children.

In our complex and sophisticated society everything is
being questioned, and simple issues are no longer seen as
simple. There is a reluctance to talk about good and evil,
about right and wrong. If as parents we demonstrate a disregard for the law – however trivial – we create confusion in
the minds of our children. The distinction between right and
wrong becomes blurred. When this happens children begin to
see the law as a matter of personal convenience and not as
something that is necessary for the safety and wellbeing of
others also. Now we can begin to see the real dangers of
regarding and treating any form of crime as trivial.

We cannot have it both ways. We cannot tell our sons and
daughters to lead honest lives and then indulge in small dis-
honesties ourselves. We cannot tell them to speak the truth
while we tell lies. Truth is not divisible, and neither is honesty.
It is the living of our daily lives by which our children judge us
and from which they take their lead. How well we succeed in
this will largely determine how good a life we have as a nation,

how free we are in the future from crime, violence and selfishness, and what kind of police service we will have.

I remain optimistic about our future. When the year 2000 arrives, I may not personally be around to greet it (although my hopes are high), but though there may have been changes by that time in policing methods and technology, I am certain that fundamentally the police service in Britain then will be little different from now. It will still operate within a democratic framework, and it will stand firm in the community on its pillars of public confidence and co-operation.

I have tried to tell you something of the philosophy and development of the modern British police service. I have discussed with you current issues which I see as likely to be with us for the next decade and more. The resolution of these issues does not lie in the hands of the police alone. As the first Commissioners made plain, the problems of policing are the problems of society as a whole, and their solution demands a joint effort between the public and their police. Certainly, police can deal with the symptoms of a situation. But what is needed is a change of attitude: a reassertion of the Christian ethic grounded in biblical truth.

As Christians, whilst we must be realists and appreciate that crime will always be with us (since man is fallen), we must not allow despair about the darker side of mankind to overcome our determination to create a better world. It is up to Christians everywhere to show how men and women can face up to their human failings, and to set an example which will encourage people to be less concerned about themselves and more concerned about others. The contemporary challenge for all Christian men and women is to learn to deny ourselves and to take up the cross of Christ (Luke 9:23).

Let me conclude by telling you a story. A father was at home looking after his young son for the day. The weather was cold and wet, and the boy was becoming increasingly bored and irritable. Hoping to keep the lad quiet for a time, dad tore out a page of the magazine he was reading on which there was a map of the world. He then tore the page into several pieces and gave it to his son. 'There you are,' he said, 'go into the other room and put that jig-saw together.'

Off went the boy, and father settled back to enjoy an hour's peace and quiet. Barely five minutes had elapsed when the boy returned with the jig-saw complete – a map of the world stuck together with sellotape.

'How ever did you manage that?' asked his father in aston-
ishment. 'Well, dad,' said the boy, 'I tried putting the world
together but it was a bit difficult. Then I found that on the
other side there was a picture of a man. So I turned all the
pieces over and stuck the man together. When I turned it back
again there was the map of the world.'

The moral is clear; if we want to put the world right, we
have to put man to rights first. This is both the heart of the
gospel and also an essential perspective for all law enforcement agencies as we face the future.

# Notes and References

1 The Metropolitan Police District covers an area of nearly 800 square miles, roughly equal to, although slightly larger than, Greater London. At 31st December 1978 the establishment of the Force was 26,589, with an actual strength of 22,197 officers. In addition, approximately fifteen thousand civil staff are employed. Within the MPD there is a resident multi-racial population of approximately eight million and an annual tourist population of about the same number again.

   The Commissioner of Police of the Metropolis (to give him his full title) is directly accountable to Parliament through the Home Secretary, who is the Police Authority (i.e. has a political and financial responsibility) for the Metropolitan Police. Other Forces in Britain have a police committee comprised of local councillors and local magistrates. The Commissioner, like all Chief Police Officers, is independent of his police authority in operational policing matters. Operational decisions are solely a police responsibility.

   Police, however, do not have an unfettered discretion. In the first place they are bound by the constraints of the law itself, and if they abuse those constraints they are liable under the law as is any other citizen. In so far as prosecutions are concerned, in the more serious cases it is the Director of Public Prosecutions who decides whether to prosecute; this of course will to some extent influence the course of police investigation into the crime. Moreover, in cases of homicide, initially police have to act and investigate under the watchful eye of the Coroner, who is legally required to hold an inquest whenever a violent, sudden or unnatural death occurs. In addition to the foregoing constraints, following the introduction of the Police Act 1976 there is now an independent element (the Police Complaints Board) which monitors the investigation of complaints against police.

   For a more detailed discussion of the constitutional position of the police see I. T. Oliver, 'The Office of Constable – 1975', *Criminal Law Review* 1975, pp. 313 et seq.

2 See 'The police: a Social Service', Maurice Punch and Trevor Naylor, *New Society*, 17th May 1973.

3 Nowadays Peel would be regarded as an outstanding administrator as well as a distinguished politician. He was, as one of his many biographers describes:

   . . . a government man. His training and family life had given his mind a colour and bias even before he entered politics. The tradition of his father and his grandfather was that of middle-class Pittite Toryism: not an inflexible and doctrinaire resistance to change, but a desire for legality and order, for evolutionary and peaceful progressivism, combined with a respect for established institutions and an old-fashioned evangelical Protestantism not far removed from that of Wilberforce and Percival. It is unlikely that Harrow or Christ Church had done anything to weaken this emotional and intellectual framework.

*Mr Secretary Peel: The life of Sir Robert Peel to 1830.* N. Gash (Harvard University Press, 1961) quoted in *Police Work: the social organisation of policing* P. K. Manning (MIT Press, 1977), p. 74.
4  *The Blind Eye of History*, Charles Reith (Faber & Faber, 1952), p. 171.
5  Ibid., pp. 171–172.
6  Ibid: see Chapter 8 'British Police Today' pp. 154–173.
7  *Metropolitan Police Instruction Book*, Chapter 1, paragraphs 2–4.
8  *Royal Commission on the Police 1962* (HMSO), Cmnd 1728. See Chapter VIII 'The Police and the Public'.
9  *The Public and the Police*, William A. Belson (Harper and Row, London, 1975).
10  See *Report of Commissioner of Police for the Metropolis*, 1978 (HMSO, 1979).
11  'What Makes People Criminals?' Article by Patricia Morgan, *Daily Telegraph*, 29th August 1978.
12  Ibid.
13  Ibid.
14  See *The Times*, 30 November 1972.
15  For a fuller discussion of the crime problem, particularly in relation to juveniles, see 'A Police Perspective', J. F. Newing, *Royal Society of Health Journal*, February 1976.
16  'Report of an Inquiry by the Hon. Sir Henry Fisher into the circumstances leading to the trial of three persons on charges arising out of the death of Maxwell Confait and the fire at 27 Doggett Road London, SE6.' (HMSO, 1977).
17  *The Growth of Crime: The International Experience*, Sir Leon Radzinowicz and Joan King (Hamish Hamilton, 1977).
18  See 'Two Treatises of Government', 1690.
19  See William Temple, *The Ethics of Penal Action*, Clarke Hall Lecture 1934.
20  Ghani v. Jones (1970) I. QB. 693.
21  *The West Indian Community*, Report of Select Committee on Race Relations and Immigration (HMSO, 1977), para 9.
22  *The Police Revolution*, Peter Evans (George Allen and Unwin, 1974), pp. 84–85.
23  Op. cit., para 149.
24  'Crime and the Young', Sir David McNee QPM, National Association of Boys Clubs, 1978.
25  Para 2. Memorandum of Police Evidence to Select Committee on Race Relations, *supra*.

26  Quoted on p. 270 of *A Force for the Future*, Roy Lewis (Temple Smith, 1976).

27  One notorious example was the Kitty Genovese case in New York in March 1964. A *New York Times* article described how:

> For more than half an hour 38 respectable, law-abiding citizens in Queens watched a killer stalk and stab a woman in three separate attacks in Kew Gardens. Twice the sound of their voices and the sudden glow of their bedroom lights interrupted and frightened him off. Each time he returned, sought her out and stabbed her again. Not one person telephoned the police during the assault; one witness called after the woman was dead.

During the course of the police investigation witnesses were asked why they had not called the police. One man said, 'I was too tired. I went back to bed.' Another said, 'I didn't want to get involved.' Although the attack started at 3.15 am the call to the police was not made until 3.50 am. The police arrived within two minutes. Whether or not they could have prevented the murder of Kitty Genovese is a moot point: the fact is they were never given the chance to find out.

28  *Evening News* 7 December 1978.

29  *Daily Mail* 16 February 1979.

30  See also Titus 3:1 f and 1 Peter 2:13 f.

31  See Job 34:12 and Deuteronomy 32:4. The book of Amos provides a good example of the Old Testament prophets' denunciation of the misuse of power.

# IV Preventing Delinquency

## Dr Bob Holman

### Introduction
Baroness Wootton, a magistrate who has dealt with over ten thousand juvenile cases, states:

> . . . juvenile delinquency has few rivals as a topic on which press and public delight to display their prejudices and to make generalizations unsupported by empirical evidence. [1]

This chapter will certainly reveal my prejudices, but I hope they will not be entirely unsupported by empirical evidence. In the first half I will consider delinquency in general. After sketching the juvenile system, I will look at some explanations of delinquency, some recent research findings and some Christian responses. In the second part, I will turn from the general to the specific, in order to describe a project on a council estate in which I am personally involved, and which hopes to prevent delinquency.

### Juvenile Delinquency: Explanations and Responses
*Delinquents and the juvenile court*
Children aged 10–14 years and young persons aged 14–17 years who offend may appear before juvenile courts.* Young adults aged 17–21 go to adult courts, but can receive certain sentences considered appropriate for youngsters. What kind of offences bring them before the juvenile courts? National figures for 1976 show that the great majority of offences involve theft or burglary, about eleven percent criminal damage and under ten percent violence against the person. [2] Priestley, Fears and Fuller's detailed study of two localities revealed that sixty percent of juvenile crimes brought to court were offences such as shoplifting, burglary and taking cars,

---

*This applies to England and Wales. A different system operates in Scotland.

which did not entail violence. In over half these cases the value of the stolen goods was less than five pounds. Between eleven and fourten percent concerned offences against property in conjunction with violence. An even smaller proportion involved damage to property, that is, vandalism.[3]

How have magistrates dealt with offenders? Priestley and his colleagues found that in Bristol 25.9 percent were fined and 13.3 percent given a conditional discharge. Apart from a fraction found not guilty, the remainder were placed on supervision, put in care of the local authority or sent to attendance or detention centres. In Wiltshire, the magistrates differed in making more use of fines and less use of attendance centres.[4] Obviously, variations occur between different sets of magistrates, but these local figures support national ones which indicate that – despite popular belief to the contrary – courts are prepared to use custodial sentences.[5] Indeed, the Howard League for Penal Reform claims that the number of young adults sent to prisons, borstals and detention centres more than doubled from 6,430 in 1961 to 15,111 in 1977, while the numbers aged 14–16 years given custodial sentences jumped from 971 to 6,997.[6]

So much for the practice of the courts. Is juvenile crime increasing? In England and Wales in 1976, 107,146 boys aged 10–17 were convicted of indictable offences* (and 64,701 were cautioned by the police). This indicates a three-fold increase since 1956.[7] However, a number of qualifications must be added.

a.  The increase is by no means consistent. For instance, between 1974 and 1976, the number of males aged 17–21 per 100,000 of the population who were convicted of indictable offences did increase. But decreases were recorded for boys aged 10–14 and 14–17 years.[8]

b.  Police manpower has increased substantially in recent years, – for instance, an increase of 12,600 between 1971–1977 – and thus an increased detection rate can be expected.[9]

c.  Delinquency should not be highlighted as the fastest growing field of crime. Over the past ten years the

* Indictable offences are serious offences triable by jury at Crown Court, whereas summary offences can go before magistrates' courts. But magistrates can try certain indictable offences if the accused foregoes the right to trial by jury.

ratio of juvenile to all crimes has remained constant at about thirty percent.[10]

d. There is a danger of comparing a present dark age with a golden Victorian Britain. In fact, Victorian Britain was characterized by complaints of rising crime rates. Moreover, according to police returns in 1859, the number of criminals in places like Birmingham and Sheffield was one in 54.4 of the population. Estimates for prostitutes and juvenile thieves were also astonishingly high.[11]

Juvenile delinquency is a serious problem, and over the last decade detected crime has increased. But care must be taken not to exaggerate its present rate, nor to gloss over what happened in past eras.

Returning to the present, who are these juvenile delinquents? Boys outnumber girls by four to one, although the recent rate of increase is greater for females.[12] Next, as Priestley, Fears and Fuller point out, '. . . most detected crime is committed by small groups of young urban working-class males.'[13] The significant words are 'detected' and 'working class'. Dr Belson's well-known survey found that over ninety percent of boys aged 13–16 admitted to stealing something.[14] Public school boys were disposed towards stealing from changing rooms and de-frauding public transport, while state school lads were more likely to steal cigarettes and sweets. But only a small minority are detected and prosecuted. Those who are tend to be working class. Even amongst these, a further fraction who must cause most concern will have two characteristics. They will continue to be delinquent, and they will progress to more serious offences such as burglary, 'muggings', car thefts and violence.

*Explanations of delinquency*

Notwithstanding the qualifications, delinquency is a serious problem. What is its cause? Let me – briefly and inadequately – outline five explanations. (These explanations cover some of the ground already discussed by Charles Colson in Chapter I, pp. 19–34, but they consider evidence with a particular bearing on delinquency among young people.)

First, *sin*. Some Christians dismiss sociological or psychological theories with 'it's all due to sin'. True, without sin there would be no crime. But, given a fallen world, this begs many questions. If all possess the capacity for evil, why do some express it in delinquency and others in cheating, hypocrisy and bad temper? Why is the sin of delinquency considered more detrimental to society than, say, tax evasion or adult motoring offences? Do certain individuals suffer from particular personalities or circumstances which predispose them towards delinquency rather than other sins?

Secondly, writers such as Professor Eysenck relate delinquency to some form of *genetic endowment.*[15] They argue not for the existence of a specific criminal gene but rather that inherited characteristics, such as aggressiveness and impulsiveness, direct some people into criminal behaviour. In support of this thinking is the reported association between criminal parents and delinquent children.[16]

My assessment is that some inherited factors do foster delinquency, but that this is not the complete or only answer. Aggression might well be inherited, but it could equally well lead to a successful and honest career in sales promotion. Further, some delinquents do not have criminal parents, while some criminals do produce law-abiding youngsters. Even where crooks beget crooks, the causal link is not necessarily genetic. The children's waywardness may spring from the likelihood that such families live in delinquent neighbourhoods or from the inadequate child rearing methods employed by the parents.

The third explanation concerns *family mal-functioning.* Ever since Bowlby's classic *44 Juvenile Thieves,*[17] an association has been postulated between delinquency and broken homes or homes with an interrupted relationship with parents. Bowlby's thesis has met much modern criticism,[18] and other psychologists and psychiatrists have focussed on the emotional relationship between children and parents, whether or not they are ever separated. They claim that an abnormal relationship distorts personality, which may then be expressed in delinquency. Andry, for instance, argued that boys liable to both over-protection from mothers and hostility to their fathers eventually projected their disturbance in antisocial ways.[19]

Some sociologists stress family mal-functioning in the form of inadequate child rearing practices. The assumption is that differing methods – the degree of parental participation in play, the kind of discipline exercised, the amount of verbal stimulation and so on – determine later behaviour. An early exponent, Spinley, considered that lower working class methods led to traits of insecurity, aggressiveness and narcissism in children who were therefore likely to become delinquents. [20] More recently, Sir Keith Joseph has added that as inadequate parents of this kind teach inadequate child raising methods to their children then they, in turn, will also become 'bad parents', so that the cycle of deprivation is perpetuated.

Modern research has cast some doubts on the cycle of deprivation theories. I have summarized these elsewhere, and here it is sufficient to say that the proponents have not considered sufficiently which factors stimulate inadequate practices. [21] Is it really that some parents do not appreciate proper child rearing methods, or is it that their circumstances push them into ways they do not want to adopt?

The mention of 'circumstances' raises a fourth explanation, which can be called *response to environment*. Its supporters agree that delinquents are the victims of outside forces, but disagree as to their nature. For instance, a well-known judge surely reflects strong popular sentiment when he blames delinquency on 'the abandonment of the moral standards handed down to us through the Christian religion and our Western culture'. [22] A more radical but still environmentalist view pinpoints the lack of opportunities open to lower working class youngsters. Thus Cohen maintains that middle class children are equipped by education and background to attain society's goals. Children not so prepared seek outlets in less legitimate ways. [23] Others describe sub-cultures where certain types of delinquency are socially acceptable. Youngsters who go shoplifting, therefore, may be just conforming to their environment. [24]

Although they possess some validity, these environmental approaches cannot explain all delinquency. For many children subjected to the decline in moral standards, to a lack of opportunities and to delinquent areas, do not become delinquents.

A fifth explanation looks at the linkage between *poverty (or social deprivation) and delinquency*. I will describe it in more detail, not because it provides a definitive answer, but because recent studies based on it are stressing the interaction between individuals, family behaviour and the environment. Poverty refers to a lack of money. Social deprivation covers others wants – inadequate housing, education, health, physical amenities, etc. However, I shall use the terms interchangeably. I accept Professor Lafitte's definition of poverty:

> . . . a level of income sufficiently low to be generally regarded as creating hardship, in terms of the community's prevailing standards, and so requiring remedial action on the part of public social policy. [25]

Lack of space does not allow a discussion of the extent of poverty today, and I can only – somewhat immodestly – refer to my recent book. [26]

Undoubtedly, a link exists between poverty and delinquency. West and Farrington, in their London survey, concluded that poverty was one of the major factors associated with juvenile crime. [27] Some of the reasons seem obvious. The poor tend to be drawn from the lower social classes – that is the Registrar General's classes IV and V – which are the ones most vulnerable to prosecution. [28] Public school thieves may well be dealt with inside their schools. Middle class estates are less subject to police patrols. Contrariwise, poor families may be known to and constantly visible to statutory authorities. Again, the poor may well be more tempted to steal in order to possess those goods which the majority take for granted. As it says in Proverbs 30:9, 'If a man is rich he may think he has no need of God, but if he is poor he may steal.'

The connection between poverty and delinquency can be much more complicated. In an important recent study, Drs Wilson and Herbert compared a sample of large, poor families with control groups. [29] Over two years, the families were subjected to educational, medical and social assessments. Here I can refer to just four general findings.

First, the low income families were far more likely to have delinquent children. Secondly, they did tend to use 'inadequate' child rearing methods. They participated less with their children, employed both repressive and permissive means of discipline, severed close child/parent relationships at an early stage, and so on. The researchers had few doubts that such practices meant that the youngsters never developed the language skills and motivation to succeed at school and work; that they never found the inner satisfactions of hobbies or crafts; that in consequence they exhibited traits of withdrawal or aggression. In short, they were being equipped with the characteristics that lead to delinquency.

Thirdly, and importantly, Wilson and Herbert discovered that the low income parents did care about their children, and did want to raise them like other families.Their inadequate methods were a reluctant adaptation to social deprivations. For instance, they could not afford the toys, games and outings which facilitate parental participation. The researchers state that

> The scarcity or total absence of toys and equipment suitable for play and the absence of privacy allowing intensive play prevent the development of creative activities, powers of concentration, manipulative skills, and the re-enactment of experiences in imaginative role play.[30]

In noisy overcrowded homes, children were early pushed on to the streets and allowed out late. In the terraced houses, peace and quiet was at a premium and parents tended to give in to children rather than risk rows which disturbed others. In the course of time, these responses to poverty became established ways of child rearing, although detrimental to their development.

Fourthly, long-term, hopeless poverty has a destructive impact. Wilson and Herbert show that there is a poorest of the poor, those who face continual ill-health, unemployment and crises about debts and evictions. The result can be a shattering of self-respect and motivation, and a resulting apathy or aggression which poisons family life. The children's upbringing suffers, and their behaviour and morals can be adversely affected. Poverty and delinquency are connected, and the major link is through the effect which poverty has on family life.

Wilson and Herbert's research and interpretation reveal how the pre-condition of poverty can upset both family and individual practices. But not all children of the poor become delinquent. Why not? I would hazard that genetic factors lead to some variations. Wilson and Herbert also point out that there are important differences in the child rearing methods which the poor may use in the face of social deprivations. One difference was of outstanding importance regarding delinquency. A minority of parents – about twenty-eight percent – reacted in an opposite way. Faced with busy roads, attacks by strangers in the neighbourhood, fears about the influence of delinquent children, they exerted extremely tight control over their school age children and hardly let them out at all. Significantly, these youngsters were much less likely to become delinquent. On the other hand, this 'chaperonage' could mean that they missed outside activities, lacked friendships, became unpopular, and suffered the restrictions of over-crowded living conditions.

Poverty is not *the* explanation of delinquency. For great variations exist in the ways the poor react to their deprivations. But Wilson and Herbert have established that poverty can channel some families into practices which make their children more vulnerable to crime than the population at large.

### Research and the response to delinquency

There is no complete explanation of delinquency. If I possessed it, I would have offered my services to the world before now! No doubt all the explanations contain elements of truth and account for some delinquency. Simultaneously, other delinquencies will result from a combination of these explanations.

Attempts to counter delinquency must be partially based on existing theories about explanations. In addition, they can also be geared to research findings about the actual practice of delinquency. Thus I will now turn to empirical studies concerning the boys' own views of their experiences: factors which tend to be associated with delinquency; what happens once youngsters are apprehended; and the effectiveness of social work intervention.

### What do the delinquents say?

One research team asked the offenders why they committed crimes.[31] Over half, 59.9 percent, frankly admitted that they stole for material gain. I too have met this response. One evening, half a dozen teenagers discussed this topic in my home and argued that as they possessed very little they were justified in stealing from the affluent. Affluence is flaunted in our society and we may underestimate the resentment of those who are excluded. One Saturday evening, a teenage boy entered my home in tears. His family exist on social security and, on going to prepare his meal, he discovered that his brothers had finished the food. He turned on me in anger, 'When you're hungry, you just have to go to your freezer – I can't.' He has committed many thefts.

Another major reason put forward – by 19.2 percent – was to escape from boredom. Again, this is an echo of the boys with whom I mix. Thus one stated, in a tape recording, 'I was with some friends, we were bored, there was some stones and some windows in an empty house, so we broke them; all this happened because we had nothing to do.' The boys were subsequently charged for this and other vandalism.

No other single reason compared in size with these two. 7.6 percent of the youngsters offered an excuse such as being drunk or too young to know what they were doing. 4.3 percent felt they had to tag along with friends.

Some light may also be shed by noting *the association between delinquency and certain factors*. Of course, not all research information of this kind is useful. One study reports a significant relationship between broken noses and delinquents.[32] Having suffered the effects of a right hook myself, I find this a sensitive subject and will pursue it no more. More interestingly, delinquency is associated with truancy. Priestley and his colleagues record that twenty percent of the offences they studied were committed during school time.[33] Delinquency is often associated with aggression. Thus West and Farrington found delinquents significantly more likely to be violent than non-delinquents.[34] Offenders do not usually act alone or in large gangs. More usually they function in pairs or small groups.[35] Delinquents are likely to have poor academic records or be in low status jobs.[36] Delinquency is associated with certain geographical localities, particularly inner ring areas or council estates, characterized by unsatisfactory housing conditions, high unemployment, early school leaving and a high proportion of manual workers.[37]

It must be stressed that the above factors are not synonymous with delinquency. Some boys will play truant, be aggressive, do badly at school, etc., and not be delinquent. However, these factors frequently do appear in conjunction, and any attempts to tackle juvenile delinquency must take them into account.

What happens once the delinquents are convicted? For some boys, an offence is a temporary break in a law-abiding career. For many others, the initial offence can lead to *recur-*

*ring delinquency*. In the sample of offenders studied by Priestley, Fears and Fuller, some forty percent had already had previous official contacts with the law.[38] West and Farrington, in following up their sample, found that sixty-one percent were subsequently re-convicted as adults. Moreover, the younger the boys were at their first offence, the greater the chance of adult law breaking.[39]

Interestingly, West and Farrington also found that the actual appearance in court was associated with further offences. They compared offenders who were prosecuted with a similar group who were not taken to court. The prosecuted group subsequently committed more crimes than the others.

Why should this happen? Court appearances bring boys into contact with other delinquents who may encourage crime. The police may get to know the convicted and keep a close watch on them thereafter. For instance, soon after his first contact with the police, a teenager was walking close to a parked vehicle. A police car stopped and the policeman who had previously arrested him, immediately accused him of intending to break into the car. He arrived at my house bitter and resentful. Another reason may be that convictions confirm to the boys the bad image they already hold of themselves. They then act – often in a boastful manner – to reinforce this image. Whatever the reasons, there is little doubt that early offences and court appearances tend to precipitate further delinquency.

So far, I have considered the delinquents, their backgrounds, and the courts. What of those social work agencies entrusted with providing *help for delinquents?* I have no time to deal with the complex modes of intervention – some very imaginative and adventurous – which now exist. Instead, let me make two points about their limitations. First, there is a limit to the effectiveness of social workers and probation officers, to whom the courts may entrust the supervision or care of offenders. Faced with large caseloads, sprawling districts, a great variety of cases, they count themselves fortunate to see their charges once a week or fortnight. Within a few minutes a week, can they really be expected to exert control or to cure a waywardness whose roots dig deep into family or community life?

Secondly, even if delinquents are sent away to institutions, the outcome is not always promising. Some successes are won, but of boys released from approved schools from 1963 to 1967, sixty-six percent were re-convicted within three years. Seventy-three percent of boys leaving detention centres and eighty-one percent from borstals re-offend within two years.[40] Some evidence even suggests that youngsters will commit more offences while in institutions than when in the community.[41] Devoted and skilled as are some residential staff, to expect them to cure difficult youths when they are removed from their neighbourhood and surrounded by other delinquents, is to expect too much of them. No wonder that even the Home Office Research Unit concluded that '. . . residential programmes are largely ineffective in reducing the incidence of subsequent delinquent behaviour.'[42]

Empirical research, then, certainly can reveal what delinquents say about themselves, and can show both that delinquency tends to recur and that present treatment methods are not highly successful. Hopefully, its findings about the factors associated with delinquency will prove of some use when it is considered what further action can be taken.

### What can be done?

Much ground has been covered in this chapter. Three deductions can be made. First, delinquency is a cause for concern. It should not be separated out as the only or the major symptom of a nation which has turned from God. But it has increased over the last decade, and it damages the delinquents themselves as well as their victims. Secondly, delinquency has no simple or single explanation. Its multiple causation will require varied means of intervention which deal with both individual personalities and their environments. Thirdly, to date, responses to delinquency – by the courts, by social workers, by Christians – have not stemmed the tide.

What then can be done? At a political and social level, I believe we should strive for *the abolition of poverty*, that is, for a more equal society. I believe that the biblical teaching about the Year of Jubilee in Leviticus 25 reveals a commitment to sharing out private resources. I believe that the New Testament recommends that while not wanting much for ourselves, we should be concerned about the material needs of others. A more equal society – not absolutely equal, for that is impossible – would mean fewer people experiencing those social deprivations which inhibit good child rearing methods, fewer suffering educational disadvantages, fewer being cut off from the rest of the population by suspicion, resentment, envy and fear. The conclusion that Wilson and Herbert draw from their classic research is that

> . . . in the final analysis the problem of disadvantaged children does not lie in genetic or psychological deficits, it lies in an unequal distribution of the resources of our society.[43]

Of course, less poverty would not mean the abolition of all delinquency. As long as sin remains, individuals will commit criminal acts – along with sins of pride, adultery, neglect and so on. But a more equal society would make some youngsters less vulnerable to delinquency, would reduce the social handicaps which can push them into crime, and would strengthen some families. The reduction of poverty will require political action. Simultaneously, it will require individual practice, which in turn will involve deciding what we do with our resources, wealth, possessions, incomes and talents.

The above proposal will strike horror and anger into the hearts of conservative readers. My next plea will be more acceptable. It is that juvenile courts must underline their role in dispensing *justice*. Some writers have argued that courts should be concerned wholly with the treatment of children or even that delinquents should be dealt with only by welfare or educational bodies.[44] My opposition is three-fold. First, such a step would blur the distinction between right and wrong. Certainly, powerful psychological, family and environmental forces may direct children towards crime, and certainly efforts should be made to understand and reduce them. But, even given these forces, crime is still wrong, and any trends which play down its seriousness may only encourage further delinquency. Secondly, my impression is that delinquents both expect and prefer justice. Thirdly, society does have the right to be protected from delinquency. This is not just a plea to preserve the peace, pockets and property of the middle classes. Frequently, working class areas suffer most from vandalism, violence, break-ins, muggings and burgled meters. Courts must take into account the welfare of children, but their prime duty is to dispense justice.

I hope that the above two suggestions create a balance between concern for the offender and for the victim, between help and punishment. Measures based on the extremes of just one of these approaches may satisfy their advocates, but will achieve little. I recall attending a Christian holiday convention at which a speaker's plea for corporal punishment and stiffer and longer sentences brought forth from the audience such rapturous cheering as would have deafened a football crowd. The enthusiasm seemed wholly for punitive measures while few voices were raised to express concern for individual delinquents. I wish members of that audience could have stood with me a few months ago to see a teenage boy being horse-whipped by his mother. He has suffered many beatings, but he continues to steal. Youngsters need affection and stability as well as discipline. Similarly, policies should not be based just on sympathy for the delinquents. If so, the youngsters may see little wrong in their acts. A balance is required between caring and control, forgiveness and retribution. A good family offers both, and social action directed towards delinquents must do likewise.

Once youngsters commit a number of offences, neither courts nor social welfare agencies have much success in changing them. A major proposal, therefore, is that more emphasis must be placed on *the prevention of crime*, on stopping youngsters ever getting to the courts or, at least, restricting them to one or two offences. Preventive programmes can be planned and need not be hit or miss affairs. They can be based on the explanations and on the factors associated with delinquency which I have outlined above. For instance, one theory of delinquency stresses an inadequate relationship with the parents, so a preventive input could involve a worker fulfilling a parental role towards a boy. Again, I have shown that boredom, aggression, truancy, group pressures, etc., can be linked with delinquency. It follows that tactics of prevention would have to counter these factors. Moreover, it is known in which geographical localities crime is most likely to occur. Prevention can be strategically planned.

I have made several proposals to combat delinquency. My next plea is for greater *Christian involvement*. Some Christian contributions have been made. The Probation Service had its origins in the Christian search for an alternative to prison.[45] And Christian agencies founded some approved schools. Further, some individuals find a Christian calling to be social workers. My impression, however, is that in general the Christian response is little different from that of the unsympathetic

public. For instance, it is not unusual to hear Christians join-
ing the conventional hypocrisy of focussing on juvenile delinquency while playing down other forms of law breaking.

Why is it that we call for tough measures against vandals but
are silent about motoring offences which are potentially more
lethal? I have even heard Christians cheerfully recounting
how they regularly exceed the speed limit. Why is delinquency
seen as the sign of a decadent society, but not the six hundred
annual deaths caused by factory accidents and negligence, or
the millions of pounds lost by tax evasion? Part of the Christian response has been to single out delinquency for condemnation.

This condemnation tends to take place from a distance. It
tends to be from the safety of the suburbs where residents
have little personal knowledge of delinquents' backgrounds,
families and feelings. Evangelical Christians may be thrilled
by stories of converted delinquents and yet be very intolerant
of the roughness and noise which lower working class lads
occasionally bring to church. There are exceptions, but frequently Christians have, on the one hand, singled out
delinquency as a special problem while, on the other hand,
isolating themselves from contact with the problem.

If more Christians were involved with delinquents, lived in
the same neighbourhoods, sent their children to the same
schools, were friends with them and their families, then they
would be simultaneously taking action and gaining understanding. Such involvement is, I believe, scriptural. The Old
Testament has many exhortations to protect and help the
needy. When Jesus Christ came, he shocked conventional
people by his readiness to mix with the poor, the disreputable
and the criminal. If the gospel is true, then surely it embraces
the delinquent. If the church is Christ-like, then surely it is not
a middle class club, but a family which can include wayward,
working class youngsters.

Delinquency is a problem. Prevention makes sense. It is
now appropriate to turn from this general discussion to one
specific example of an attempt to prevent delinquency.

**Preventing delinquency: a community project**
After several years in academic life, I was convinced of two
things. One was that I had removed myself from those in
greatest need. Every work day, I travelled from my suburban
home to teach others about social problems. The other was

that prevention was possible, but that its effectiveness was reduced because many social workers did not possess sufficient time to help, and, moreover, tended to live well away from their clients. A scheme was devised which I called community social work. Its objectives were to attempt:

> to prevent family break-ups.
> to reduce delinquency.
> to provide community facilities.

The approach was to emphasize:

> the use of a variety of social methods – individual
>   casework, group work and community work.
> concentration on a small neighbourhood.
> the worker living in or near the work area.

Two trusts funded the idea over a three-year period while the Church of England Children's Society agreed to administer it. Consequently, the project also undertook to carry out certain child care functions – particularly concerning adoption and fostering – should they be required in the area. Thus, in 1976, I left university and moved into a private house adjacent to a council estate.

*Why this estate?*
As shown in the previous section, areas of delinquency or potential delinquency can be identified. The small estate where the project was established had a high proportion of manual workers and an above-average number of one parent families. It also scored high on indices such as number of offences and children taken into care. In addition, it was separated from the city centre by expensive bus fares, had no council youth clubs, no community association, no café and only one shop. This is not to say that it was an untypical council estate. Indeed, it was hoped that the project would demonstrate its effectiveness in a locality not unlike thousands of others. Not least, the estate was chosen because I already knew some of its residents and had discussed the idea with them.

*The start*
The project began with one worker – myself – and no premises, save my house. What a tinpot outfit! How could I start?

My initial priorities had to be to meet people and assess need.

The focal point of the estate is one all-purpose shop. Within this unofficial community centre, a bevy of housewives orchestrate initiation ceremonies for newcomers. A woman, standing behind a pile of tins, suddenly shouted, 'Bob, help, I've got me boob stuck in the corned beef.' All eyes turned on me. Dignified silence was out of the question, as was any thought of removing the aforementioned part of her unmentionables. Instead, I replied, 'Sorry, I don't like touching bad meat.' The resulting laughter has been followed by continuing daily banter. As, also, my wife has that kind of Glaswegian accent which is accepted anywhere, the seeds were planted for some significant relationships.

Simultaneously, I was knocking at every door on the two main roads, both to explain the project and to ask residents what they thought needed doing. I noticed delinquency, truancy, some unemployment, children's bewilderment when a new 'parent' moved in, and low incomes. Residents also saw these problems, but the one on which they urged me to take action concerned youngsters in the streets. Apparently, they rode motor bikes, threw stones, played football and were rowdy until late at night. I dawdled on the streets to talk to the youngsters, sometimes feeling uneasy as they encircled me. Eventually, a number approached me, complaining that there was nothing to do. We met at my house and discussed their complaints and those of the adults. It was decided to start a youth club with a local resident, Dave Wiles, as chairman. The project was about to gain its identity, and Dave was later to join me as a full-time worker.

*Alternatives to delinquency*
Youth work developed as a major part of the project. It has three sections – clubs as an alternative to delinquency, group experiences and availability to individuals.

It will be remembered that some offenders attribute their actions to boredom (see p. 102). It was this very complaint that youngsters brought to me. Many are not doing well at school; they spend much time on the streets. Although some parents supervise closely, others allow children out at all hours. If they do not find legitimate outlets, they may turn to illegitimate pursuits. Boys told me of the excitement of shoplifting, of the glamour of being chased. Much time can be spent in planning a break-in, and even more in basking in the glory afterwards. Pleasure can be gained from smashing empty houses, crashing the vehicles left for the night by workmen, or setting fire to vans.

Of course, boredom can never be a complete explanation. As I have shown earlier, behind it may be the years of poverty resulting in inadequate child rearing practices, which do not develop children's abilities to amuse themselves in reading or craft. Broken families may mean that a lone parent is too stretched to keep contact with her children for long periods. Whatever the cause, the expression becomes boredom, a boredom which is not modified in an area which has no official play space, football pitch or amenities.

It follows that the request for a youth club fitted into the project's intention to reduce delinquency by countering boredom. Three years later, a winter week sees the project running a senior club, two junior clubs and activities on Saturdays. During the summer these are supplemented by camps, holidays and play projects. The clubs are held in various church halls. Membership is usually limited to about forty because we (I now use 'we' as Dave Wiles joined the project after one year) recognize that clubs must be small enough to allow a relationship between leaders and youngsters. The clubs have three major roles:

i   to be facilities which youngsters regard as their own. Unless members possess loyalty towards the clubs, then facilities can simply be the arena for more boredom and vandalism.

ii  to promote some concern for others. A boy called, all steamed up about the low wages paid in sheltered workshops. A sheltered workshop is situated near the estate and one handicapped man is well known to us. After discussion with him, it was agreed to buy a specially adapted washing machine. With the help of parents, the necessary £130 was raised. The youngsters discovered that for all their disadvantages, they too could help others. Not least, the resulting local publicity gave them (and others) a new, more positive image of themselves.

iii to provide activities which are interesting but not delinquent. The clubs are very ordinary, with the usual snooker, table tennis and records. But they do supply the minimum of a warm place to mix with friends. Some of the members would never get into trouble anywhere. But for others, the clubs serve as a diversion from temptations which may involve crime. Certainly, the clubs do hold a number of boys who are on the fringe of delinquency. The activities do not remove the root cause, but if they help to reduce some court appearances by a handful of vulnerable teenagers, then a positive contribution has been made.

*Group experiences*

The youth clubs have given a fixed framework to the project. But some youngsters can become unduly aggressive or withdrawn in the club setting. Further, as mentioned, delinquents often operate in pairs or in small groups. The project, therefore, has established some flexible groups of between four and fourteen youngsters, in which they can feel at ease and yet still be diverted from delinquency.

Diversion, in our view, is most likely to occur if the groups contain both offenders and non-offenders. One of the disadvantages of a statutory social worker gathering together the delinquents on his caseload is that the norms and influences of the group become predominantly delinquent. Community social workers, however, because they work with a neighbourhood rather than a particular set of clients, can draw upon a wide range of youngsters and thus construct more balanced groups.

Early on, we became especially concerned about the problems of the boys most vulnerable to long-term public care – those from one-parent families.[46] To form a group just of such youngsters would immediately have singled them out as the Bastards' Group or some similar unpleasant name. Instead, we invited six one-parent boys to come and also to bring a friend. The group meets once a week starting with ordinary indoor games followed by refreshments and discussion.

This weekly group is supplemented by more *ad hoc* ones. Often we will take half a dozen boys swimming or to table tennis. Trips to speedway or football may end up with chips and chat in the van. During the summer, camps provide the opportunity for group members to live with each other for a few days.

The group activities may be enjoyable or exhausting – but do they help? As members have got to know us, so it has become easier to promote *discussions*. In the group which

includes one-parent boys we directly face the painful questions of what it's like without dad, what pressures weigh on
mum, what are the dangers of truancy, and so on. Within
these debates, we put forward our view. Thus, when an informal group argued in my kitchen that their lack of money
justified theft, our contribution was to acknowledge the evil of
inequality, but to deny that it legitimized delinquent behaviour. Interestingly, the group itself then admitted that the
consequences of being caught – loss of freedom – were out of
proportion to the material gains from stealing.

Talking is not enough. Groups can also *introduce new
experiences*. Consider our ordinary provision of outings and
holidays. Despite the myth that the working class spend their
holidays in Spain, the Social Tourism Study reported that
most low income families have no holiday whatsoever.[47]
Certainly, most youngsters we take away would not otherwise
have a holiday. One day we took six on the seventy-minute
train trip to London. Five of the six had never been to London
before. A Christian friend has given some lads training and
qualifications in trampolining. An interest amongst younger
boys in bird watching has been encouraged by trips to bird
reserves. We hope that these new experiences lead to legitimate interests which occupy the boys.

New experiences can also promote *greater self-confidence*,
the lack of which often seems to hold back local youngsters.
My colleague took a group to a community print shop where
they were taught how to design and print Christmas cards.
New skills were acquired. Once a year we use video equip-
ment. Our group decided to act out shoplifting, with members
acting the parts of shop manager, police, magistrates, parents,
probation officer and delinquent. They gained some appreci-
ation of being in the other person's shoes, but equally
important, they developed the confidence not only to write
and act, but also to show the results to their parents and
friends.

Groups are also settings in which the youngsters' actual
*responses* to situations can be explored. Take the matter of
aggression, which is so frequently associated with delinquency. While camping, a few teenagers tried to enter a bingo
hall. The doorman told them to clear off. Their reaction was
aggression. Later at camp, there was the chance to have a
play-back, to examine their response and to explore alternative ways of meeting rejection.

Of course, the outcome of groups is not always so happy. Groups can be destructive. They can isolate and scapegoat one member. We have failed to incorporate two boys into any group. But, overall, our experiences suggest that small groups are a means of reaching and influencing needy youngsters.

*Availability to individuals*
Important as are the influences of environment and groups, most theorists of delinquency would agree that individual behaviour is strongly moulded through personal relationships. Thus, the third aspect of our youth work has been to form close friendships with about ten youngsters. They approach our home when in need. A boy rows with his family and storms out – to us. Mid-evening in winter, a youngster stands outside: alone in his house, the electricity has run out again and he has no money for the meter; he comes for warmth and shelter. 10.30 pm one Sunday evening, a familiar figure stands outside, but this time his face is stained with blood, one tooth hangs out; he has been beaten up by an older brother. These particular incidents stand out. More frequently – indeed almost every day – they come because there is nowhere else to go. One boy called five times on Christmas Day.

Within these contacts, we talk about football, pop music, the club and so on. At a deeper level, we are focussing on problems of aggression, delinquency, truancy and family relationships. Here are two examples.

*John* is sixteen, a delinquent and truant from a troubled home. Our friendship developed as he took charge of the youth club cafés. He calls every day. The Saturday I prepared these notes, he arrived at 11.30 am and stayed until 5.30 pm. The ties of trust and affection enable him to accept my checking up on his nicking and truancy. His school co-operates, and when John recently got out of control in class, a teacher brought him to us to cope for the rest of the day. Subsequently, he spent two days a week on day release with the project, on condition that he attended school on the other days. Despite some 'blow-ups', it worked well. He is a willing worker and is good at handling younger children.

*Jef* is from a one-parent family. His mother struggles hard, but he lacks the control of a father. He reacts to any frustration with aggression, even violence. At one outing, he became so out of hand – stealing, fighting, running away – that I had to pursue and restrain him physically. A passing motor cyclist then wanted to fight me because I was abusing him! Eventually, we dragged him to the van and forcibly took him home. He has already committed one serious offence, and neighbours continually complain about his destruction, bullying and foul mouth. He copes best in very small groups and can be articulate, intelligent and even charming. We have maintained friendship with him for three years, but are not yet close enough for him to tolerate much discussion of what is going wrong.

What do we offer individuals? Practical services like getting them to school. For some, we are father figures able to give the time and concern which may influence their behaviour. Not least, by developing their capacities we hope to change their negative self-image. For often the boys accept that they are society's losers who will inevitably be failures, rejects and delinquents.

*Community involvement*

As well as individual youngsters, some social work also occurs with families. Beyond families, there are activities embracing the neighbourhood as a whole.

Shortly after the project started, the council closed the only official piece of play space because of vandalism. In response, we met with some angry mums and decided to run a play scheme. A grant was obtained from the local authority, and it ran successfully during the summer holidays attracting over a hundred children. The following year the mothers virtually took over the junior part of the scheme themselves. A similar pattern developed in other activities. Bank holiday events and Christmas parties, for instance, were initiated by us and then taken over.

What is the relevance of community involvement? In the first half of this paper, it was mooted that delinquents had been adversely affected by their social situations, by the treatment received from the community. Hopefully, the activities just described help to modify this trend by encouraging a sense of local responsibility for children. Of course, certain families in the area have always shown kindness to other people's children. Our role has been to stimulate more organized efforts and to incorporate a wide range of families. Within these efforts, no children have been excluded, whatever their reputation or behaviour. The intention is that they benefit not only from the activities but also from the sense of caring that the community has for them.

A related gain may stem from the fact that the community activities identify the project with a wide variety of children and not just with delinquents. It follows that boys can be associated with the project without being labelled or written off as delinquents. Hopefully, therefore, they do not feel pressurised into proving that they are young criminals.

Community provision is closely related to participation by individual residents. Involvement is necessary because they are the persons most knowledgeable about local needs and resources; because they may well be better fitted than out-siders to communicate with neighbours; and because involve-ment may help individuals to deal with their own problems. Two specific examples can be given. Dave Wiles has spent most of his life on this council estate. As a teenager, he was into crime and violence. Eventually he was straightened out, developed concern for his neighbourhood and was elected first chairman of the youth club. Seeing his capacities, I was able to raise the cash to employ him as a full-time worker. Over the past year and a half, Dave has proved a tremendous asset. Having been through the same experiences as many of the youngsters, Dave is on their wavelength. The other example concerns the youngsters themselves. During the summer schemes, between six and eight teenagers have regularly taken on leadership roles in regard to younger children. Their involvement not only diverts them from less constructive activities, but promotes attitudes of caring for others.

*Advantages of community social work*
We are nearing the end of the first three years of the project. What advantages does this approach – working from the grass roots and living on the spot – seem to offer?

Local authority social workers are frequently helpful, but often they are not easily reached or known. From our estate, a family of four would pay £1.90 to travel to and from the Social Services Department in town before asking for an unknown official. Little wonder that people in need may not approach social workers. By contrast, the workers on our project have been easily *identifiable*. Frequently on the streets, dealing with scores of children, visiting the same shop and schools, we soon became known. Thus referrals are easily made. The shopkeeper leans over the counter to say a teenager has taken an over-dose. A mother stops me in the street to say her son, who has been in trouble, did not arrive home until the early hours of the morning.

Another advantage is that the workers can *respond quickly*. A mother complains one morning that her teenage son has barricaded himself in the loft and will not go to school. Within a few minutes I am standing on the banisters pushing trap-door and boy to one side. Eventually I got him to school and sorted out the problem. The shopkeeper complains that his paraffin vending machine has been vandalized and a part stolen. Within a short time, the culprit is found and the part returned before the police have to be involved. A man and his daughter knock on the door complaining of being harassed and attacked by some boys on the rampage – who also gather outside. I invite them in and suggest some diversions.

Workers who live in the neighbourhood are well placed to gather information about families and to *understand local dynamics*. During one week, we reckon to see over a hundred children at the clubs as well as meeting them and their parents in the streets. During the summer, we holiday with at least thirty-five youngsters. My children go to the local school. We possess, therefore, some advantages in assessing the family conflicts, the friendship patterns, the relationships at school, the emotional and financial hardships, which may explain individual acts of delinquency.

In addition, this close involvement and knowledge have now been spread over a longish period. *Trust and confidence have had time to be established*, and youngsters (and parents) become more ready to discuss personal difficulties. I recall two inhibited teenagers suddenly voicing their fears about their own lack of control, the girl about sexual behaviour, the boy about his temper. I do not think they could have done so unless we had offered them a close, long-term relationship.

Not least, mixing daily with the neighbourhood, the workers' *values become very explicit*. For instance, youngsters know that if they approach us during school time we will try to take them back to school. As the local policeman is invited to our clubs, it is clear that we are not against the police. Simultaneously, we respect individual confidences. When boys confess crimes to us, we persuade them to tell the victim, to inform the police themselves or to let us do so. But we will not 'shop' them. When two boys on the run sought refuge at our youth club, we refused, advised them to return, but did no more. After a few hours, they requested my colleague to take them back. By our actions, we hope to show a dual commitment, on the one hand upholding the law and on the other being ready to respect and accept individuals.

A community social worker is exposed to his constituency. We can be seen under stress and pressure. Our tempers, irritabilities, weak spots, sense of humour, likes and dislikes are revealed. The quality or poverty of our lives is assessed. But we are Christians. Indeed, our basic value is Christianity. How does this affect the project?

### A Christian project?
Dave Wiles and I are both Christians by conversion. We both have a commitment to share Christianity with the kind of people we were raised amongst. I came from a non-Christian family and know something of the alienating experience of being a Christian amongst working class people. More dramatically, Dave was a thief, vandal and heavy drinker. Probation had little effect on him. Then he walked into a crusade and walked out a Christian. The week before he had burgled an old lady's home. He now broke in again – to return the loot.

Despite our personal beliefs, one church refused our request to use its hall for a youth club on the grounds that the project was not fully Christian. Certainly, its objectives do not specify evangelical doctrines. Nonetheless, we believe that to offer services in Christ's name to the needy is Christian, whether the persons become Christians or not. Consequently, most of our activities do not oblige participants to attend Sunday meetings. The exception concerns Jucos (Junior Covenanters), membership of which does involve a Sunday meeting. Even so, our mid-week Jucos' club is matched by clubs offering similar activities without the Sunday stipulation. Interestingly, Jucos is so popular as to have a waiting list.

People tend to know that we are Christians, and our close relationships provide opportunities to focus on Christianity. A school-girl mother, asking me about child baptism, went on to ask about my beliefs. When some teenagers asked Dave why he did not sleep with his girl friend, he replied from a Christian perspective. A few youngsters have become Christians and then face a difficult period. It may be considered soft to stop nicking, cissy to attend church, manly to go drinking. Estate boys seem uncomfortable and unaccepted in conventional churches. We tend to take them to a small chapel where a local resident has a wonderful gift of informal communication. We are encouraged to see boys battling to stop thieving, praying to control aggression.

Is it necessary to become a Christian to avoid crime? No, although all people do need Christ to put them right with God. Some youngsters may be diverted from delinquency because, say, a non-Christian acts as a loving father figure towards them. Nonetheless, we sometimes look into other young faces which are so evil, so destructive, so bitter, that we believe that only divine intervention can alter them. As a Christian project, we want to offer the so-called secular services and also point to the Lord.

Whether outsiders regard the project as Christian or not, we feel that our reliance has to be on the Lord. The hours are long, the questions baffling, the demands unceasing. Thus, Dave and I often start the day together in prayer. In times of crisis, the prayers are clearly answered. One night I received a summons to a home where I had to remove two children from an armed and violent psychopath. I prayed as I went, for I am not a brave person. The Lord gave me an unusual calmness and firmness which resolved the situation. More commonly, we face the disappointments of boys who steal from us, the sense of failure when they do not respond, the sheer exhaustion of coping with difficult clubs until late at night. It is then that we can draw upon the Lord to be refreshed. After three years, we have a sense of being in the right place. We are convinced that to be alongside delinquents is a part of the work of Christ's followers.

*Failure and success*

Finally, is the project successful? I am acutely aware of its insignificance. The evening before composing this paragraph, I sat with a family of six who cannot cope with just Supplementary Benefit. I wanted to ask if the boys could have plimsolls for club and boots for football, but there was no point. The wife handed me an eviction notice (they were sixty pounds in rent arrears) and a bailiff's warrant to remove their cooker. The husband shouted that rather than let the kids – including a six-month-old baby – go without a cooker, he would break into the meter, even though he did have a suspended prison sentence hanging over him. Crushed into the one living room, I looked at the boys' faces as they took in the despair and wondered if I would soon be dealing with their delinquency. And I felt so useless, so powerless to change the unemployment, low income, overcrowding, which grinds families down. .Against these structural difficulties, the project is like putting band-aid on cancer.

Of course, two community social workers cannot be expected to tackle structural problems even if these do provoke delinquency. But there are also organizational failings. By concentrating on teenage boys, we sometimes neglect parents and girls. Even the number of boys whom we see intensively is small. Our clubs are not open every night, and the estate still lacks a permanent building. We are not attacking the roots of delinquency; at best we accompany some teenagers through a vulnerable period in their lives.

The limitations have been starkly stated in order to counter the tendency of practitioners to exaggerate their own contributions. Now some more positive conclusions can be suggested.

First, has the project prevented youngsters committing offences or coming into public care? The difficulty here is to establish cause and effect. A number have appeared before the courts, but only one boy has been removed (and he is now back home again). However, the outcome may not be due to us but to the efforts of school teachers or even the sentencing policy of magistrates. More specifically, we can point to examples which we do appear to have influenced. A boy was trying car doors until one opened; he hesitated, looked up, saw my house, and fled inside and out of temptation. A teenager was persuaded to meet two mates to steal a motor bike; at the appointed hour, he was too afraid to say no to them and instead asked if he could stay with me; meantime, I nipped out and cut off the other two. A youngster with a severe truancy problem has been got back to school by actually taking him and by letting him come to my house at lunch-time. All these boys have records, and a further offence could entail a custodial sentence. Noticeably, two have now completed supervision orders without serious re-convictions (although both had minor traffic offences). In these cases, delinquent tendencies are not abolished, rather they are absorbed. The examples, we admit, depend on our subjective judgment. More objectively, teachers at the local comprehensive school report that the project is having a positive effect on some of their more difficult pupils.

Secondly, we argue that the project is justified if it offers services which would not otherwise be available. More affluent sections of society have access to youth clubs, holidays, play facilities, sport and individual counselling. On the grounds of equality, we believe it right to maintain them on this estate.

Thirdly, perhaps the most important judgment is whether local residents feel we have anything to contribute. We have sounded local opinion by distributing a newspaper and then visiting every home. Of course, the residents were responding directly to us – somewhat biased interviewers – nonetheless, the overwhelming response was one of approval. Further, some of the parents and boys themselves are convinced that the project has reduced their delinquency. Dave and I share this belief, and we are committed to continuing to work amongst delinquents on this estate.

# Notes and References

1 B. Wootton, *Crime and Penal Policy* (Allen & Unwin, 1978), p. 152.
2 Joint Working Party, *The Children & Young Persons Act 1969*, table 5, p. 27.
3 P. Priestley, D. Fears and R. Fuller, *Justice for Juveniles* (Routledge & Kegan Paul, 1977), p. 45.
4 Op. cit., p. 93.
5 See C.S.O., *Social Trends No.9, 1977*, H.M.S.O., table 14.9, p. 205.
6 Cited in *The Guardian*, 2nd September, 1978.
7 Joint Working Party, op. cit., pp. 3 & 23.
8 Op. cit., table 2, p. 24.
9 C.S.O., op. cit., table 14.17, p. 209.
10 Op. cit., p.3.
11 See J. J. Tobias, *Nineteenth Century Crime: Prevention and Punishment* (David & Charles, 1972). Similar concern has been expressed throughout the ages '. . . eighteenth century commentators were thoroughly alarmed by what they saw as a rising tide of violent criminality; and complaints of the imminent breakdown of law and order punctuated the Middle Ages,' J. S. Cockburn, *Crime in England 1550–1800* (Methuen, 1977), p. 49.
12 P. Priestley, D. Fears and R. Fuller, *Justice for Juveniles* (Routledge & Kegan Paul, 1977), p. 46.
13 Op. cit., p. 97.
14 W. Belson, *Juvenile Theft: The Causal Factors* (Harper & Row, 1975).
15 H. Eysenck, *The Inequality of Man* (Temple Smith, 1973), chapter 5.
16 See H. Wilson, 'Juvenile Delinquency, Parental Criminality and Social Handicap', *British Journal of Criminology*, vol. 15, 1975.
17 J. Bowlby, *44 Juvenile Thieves* (Tindall & Cox, 1946).
18 For a review, see M. Rutter & N. Madge, *Cycles of Disadvantage* (Heinemann, 1976), chapter 6.
19 R. Andry, *Delinquency and Parental Pathology* (Methuen, 1960).
20 B. Spinley, *The Deprived and the Privileged* (Routledge & Kegan Paul, 1953).
21 R. Holman, *Poverty: Explanations of Social Deprivation* (Martin Robertson, 1978) chapter 3.
22 Cited in *The Guardian*, 2nd September, 1978.
23 A. Cohen, *Delinquent Boys: the Culture of the Gang* (Routledge & Kegan Paul, 1956).
24 J. Mays, *Growing Up In The City* (Liverpool University Press, 1954).

25  F. Lafitte, 'Income Deprivation' in R. Holman (ed) *Socially Deprived Families in Britain* (Bedford Square Press, 1970), p. 7.
26  R. Holman, *Poverty: Explanations of Social Deprivation* (Martin Robertson, 1978).
27  D. J. West and D. P. Farrington, *The Delinquent Way of Life* (Heinemann, 1977).
28  For a discussion of social class, see R. Holman, op. cit., pp. 189–193.
29  H. Wilson and G. Herbert, *Parents and Children in the Inner City* (Routledge & Kegan Paul, 1978).
30  H. Wilson and G. Herbert, op. cit., p. 185.
31  D. J. West and D. P. Farrington, *The Delinquent Way of Life* (Heinemann, 1977), p. 34.
32  D. J. West and D. P. Farrington, op. cit., p. 70.
33  P. Priestley, D. Fears & R. Fuller, op. cit., p. 46.
34  D. J. West and D. P. Farrington, op. cit., p. 82.
35  P. Priestley, D. Fears & R. Fuller, op. cit., p. 49.
36  D. J. West and D. P. Farrington, op. cit., p. 66.
37  H. Wilson and G. Herbert, op. cit., p. 76.
38  P. Priestley, D. Fears and R. Fuller, op. cit., p. 49.
39  D. J. West and D. P. Farrington, op. cit., p. 17.
40  Joint Working Party, op. cit., p. 4.
41  New Approaches to Juvenile Crime, *Sending Young Offenders Away*, 1979.
42  D. Cornish and R. Clarke, *Residential Treatment and Its Effects on Delinquency*, HMSO, 1975.
43  H. Wilson and G. Herbert, op. cit., p. 198.
44  For example, B. Wootton, op. cit.
45  See A. F. Young and E. T. Ashton, *British Social Work in the Nineteenth Century* (Routledge & Kegan Paul, 1956), pp. 172–182.
46  J. Packman, *Child Care: Needs and Numbers* (Allen & Unwin, 1969).
47  Cited in *The Guardian*, 19th August, 1975.

# V Prison: its reform and its alternatives

Michael Jenkins

## Introduction
The title of this chapter implies that something is wrong with prisons. But I desire neither to bury them nor to praise them. If anyone is to take away a man's liberty – as judge, gaoler or simply as a member of a democracy – he must consider his action conscientiously. Twenty years' experience in penal establishments makes it no easier for me! There are many dilemmas for worker and citizen, and I plan to examine some of them after setting out the context and a Christian perspective. The chapter concludes with possibilities of change, though none is 'official', since I contribute with the permission but not the authority of the Prison Department.

## An historical perspective
There have been prisons for a long time. Several are mentioned in the Bible. Joseph was put in Pharaoh's prison when he displeased Potiphar's wife (Gen. 39:20). Jeremiah was locked up as a defector (Jer. 38:6–13) and John the Baptist for treason (Matt. 14:3). In England, both lay and ecclesiastical authorities had prisons, and I need spend little time on them.[1] Oxford Prison was built on part of the ground of Oxford Castle. The records indicate that in 1577 there was an outbreak of gaol fever during the trial of a 'saucy foul-mouthed bookseller' named Rowland Jenkes (so far as I know, not one of my forebears). The Judge, the High Sheriff and three hundred other people died (Hassall, 1971). John Howard (1777) exposed the evils of these medieval prisons, for which the local justices were responsible. In the century that followed central government increasingly took the initiative to build sanitary convict prisons, appoint inspectors, approve rules, set building standards and finally to take over all the prisons. This was not an unequivocal act of moral or social determination, however, but the fulfilment of an election

pledge by Disraeli to relieve the burden on local taxpayers. It was not the only time that economic necessity has given us the courage to do the right thing.

Indeed, the Victorians were not without courage; they drastically reduced the number of capital offences at a time when crime was increasing and transportation ceased. Because of the concern for control (under the lasting influence of the French Revolution) a lot of money was spent on providing the prisons with single cells of reasonable proportions and often with sanitation. They believed in the silent system and built cells that could house men with the minimum of communication and contamination. While we might look askance at the resulting buildings, they represented a significant and costly change in attitude.

It was Du Cane who drew all the prisons together into a single system within a few years of nationalization in 1878. He closed many prisons, either because they were not needed or because they were not worth refurbishing. This eliminated sites in such desirable places as Taunton, Knutsford, Worcester and Warwick. Prison was for isolation, repentance and punishment, and Du Cane 'cleaned up' the system and the organization. But when this process had been safely completed, people began to ask the more difficult question why men returned to offending upon their release. Consequently, the Gladstone Committee on the prison system (HMSO, 1895) recommended treatment and training, so that men should leave prison better than when they went in. The adoption of this policy retrieved ideas first tried at the beginning of the nineteenth century (Webbs, 1922) and gave the impetus for a 'Golden Age' which might have continued until today had it not been shown that, overall, the treatment and training offered made no obvious difference to reconviction rates.

The 'Golden Age' introduced desirable innovations – probation, more humane regimes, more attention to prisoners' needs – and produced giants like Paterson, Llewellyn and Fox, who helped change attitudes and approaches (Fox, 1952). It was Llewellyn who led the march from Feltham closed borstal, in order to found Lowdham Grange, the first open borstal, and who subsequently opened North Sea Camp and Hewell Grange. Paterson, as secretary of the Prison Commission, lent his inspiration, support and advocacy to a system strongly committed to the training of borstal boys. Their success led in time to the embracing of therapeutic community ideals and the extension of treatment and training in prisons.

With more delinquent offenders, however, they were less successful. Criticism arose. For example, Malcolm Brown wrote in 1969: 'We will be aware of the varying philosophies underlying the enforced separation of the offender from society, namely expiation, restitution, retribution, deterrence, prevention and reformation. It is the conflict that inevitably arises once these philosophies are put into action, so to speak, that largely accounts for what one can only describe as the abysmal failure of the British Penal System. If we examine the implication of these philosophies, clearly they cannot be merged into one unified category.'[2]

Researchers raised serious questions about the effect and the effectiveness of institutions in general (e.g. Goffman, 1961 and Barton, 1966) and of penal institutions in particular (Hood, 1965 and Warder, 1973). The final blows were dealt by Martinson (1974) in the United States and Brody (1976) in England. Martinson's general conclusion was that 'with few and isolated exceptions, the rehabilitative efforts that have been reported so far have no appreciable effect on recidivism'. Of course what helps one man may not help another. Adams (1970) reported that 'amenable' delinquents succeeded better following social casework, but the same treatment offered to non-amenable delinquents in the same institution resulted in worse recidivism. Even this promising possibility with the 'amenable' has produced little. The intensive treatment offered at Grendon Underwood Prison did not lead to better success rates (Newton, 1971). In fact, the possibility of 'treatment' is seriously doubted (Leach, 1968 and Bean, 1978).

Research requires us to be realistic and to re-examine the use of imprisonment. The Prison Department is (despite the doubts of many) well aware of the current questioning and tension. It has tried to be realistic in its statement of the aims of imprisonment in *Prisons and the Prisoner* (HMSO, 1977):

The three main purposes of custodial care may be summarized as follows:
a.  To provide various services to the courts.
b.  To undertake the secure and humane containment of those committed to custody.
c.  Within the currency of their sentences, to do every-

thing possible by way of treatment and training to provide controlled conditions in which offenders can move towards a better understanding of themselves, and learn to accept and deal responsibly with the consequences of their own behaviour (*paragraph 13*).

One of the most senior staff in the Prison Department made some even more realistic assessments in the Department's centenary year:

  i. That degradation is still with us and is felt by prisoners and staff.
 ii. That the prison service is scapegoated for failing with prisoners when it would be more honest if the community had more realistic expectations and played a more constructive part.
iii. That accusations of secrecy are unfair, people did not honestly wish to hear or understand; and
 iv. That management of men and the system takes considerable skill which is not acknowledged. (Neale, 1978)

Much constructive work has been done in the past century. Relationships are, with a few exceptions, vastly improved. Regimes are more constructive and humane. Yet, generally speaking, better prospects of success elude us, or rather our charges. With more than 42,000 prisoners in custody in England and Wales, and with staff too few and anxieties high, many were glad to see the setting up of Mr Justice May's Inquiry into the work of the Prison Department. Its report, due late in 1979, may usher in as much change as was introduced by John Howard or the Gladstone Committee.

## A Christian perspective on prison

*(a) What does the Bible say?*
I am very thankful that Chuck Colson has already spoken about the origins of sin (Chapter I, pp. 34–36) and that Sir Norman Anderson has covered the biblical authority for punishment (Chapter II, pp. 50–55). I will therefore focus on imprisonment, which is usually recorded in the Bible as a hard

fact of life. We find Jesus counting as righteous those who visited him vicariously in prison (Matthew 25:36) and the writer of Hebrews urging his readers to remember those in prison 'as if chained to them', that is, as if they were their fellow prisoners (Hebrews 13:3). But Jesus groups those in prison with others who are oppressed or in need, the hungry, the naked, the sick and the stranger. While imprisonment today is given as a result of a legal judgment, and is not used as an executive instrument of control, as it was in Jesus' day, for example in the case of John the Baptist, nevertheless we should remember that Jesus links the needy together as the beneficiaries of his Messianic mission:

> He stood up to read the Scriptures and was handed the book of the prophet Isaiah. He unrolled the scroll and found the place where it is written, 'The Spirit of the Lord is upon me, because he has chosen me to bring good news to the poor. He has sent me to proclaim liberty to the captives and recovery of sight to the blind, to set free the oppressed and announce that the time has come when the Lord will save his people.' Jesus rolled up the scroll, gave it back to the attendant and sat down. All the people in the synagogue had their eyes fixed on him and he said to them 'This passage of Scripture has come true today, as you heard it being read.' (Luke 4:16–21).

It is a matter of debate among Christians whether Christ's promised freedom from oppression is political or spiritual. In my view to interpret it either way exclusively is too limiting. For both seem to be promised in the Scriptures.

Paul certainly wrote of our liberation from sin and guilt: 'God rescued us from the power of darkness and brought us safe into the kingdom of his dear Son, by whom we are set free, that is, our sins are forgiven' (Colossians 1:13–14).

But the Psalms often remind us that God has political and humanitarian interests as well. For example, 'Don't put your trust in human leaders, no human being can save you . . . Happy is the man who has the God of Jacob to help him and who depends on the Lord his God, the Creator of heaven, earth and sea, and all that is in them. He always keeps his promises; he judges in favour of the oppressed and gives food to the hungry. The Lord sets prisoners free and gives sight to the blind. He lifts those who have fallen; he loves his righteous people. He protects the strangers who live in our land; he helps widows and orphans, but ruins the plans of the wicked' (Psalm 146:3, 5–9).

This statement that God is the liberator of the oppressed presents us with a dilemma. He promises to frustrate the wicked and to free those in prison, yet the wicked flourish and prisons remain full. How can we resolve this apparent discrepancy? Surely by remembering that only in God's perfect kingdom will his promises be completely fulfilled. Meanwhile, God is patient with us. Just as he allowed the Israelites a king, though their request implied a rejection of his kingship (1 Samuel 8), and just as, according to Jesus, Moses permitted divorce because of the hardness of human hearts (Mark 10:5), so it seems that God is tolerant of our imperfect structures. This is no excuse, however, for acquiescing in them as if they were his ideal. They are not. They are only second best. And Christians should never think of them as a satisfactory substitute for the direct, loving relationships which God offers us through his Son. I see prisons as one example of those second-best structures and not as our Father's primary will.

It is true that, as is written in Romans 13 (discussed further in Chapters II and III), God approves of benevolent authority; he expects his people to obey the law and not to bring Christ's name into disrepute. Temple (1976 edition) wisely wrote: 'The most fundamental requirement of any political and economic system is not that it shall express love, though that is desirable, nor that it shall express justice, though that is the first ethical demand to be made upon it, but that it shall supply some reasonable measure of security against murder, robbery and starvation'.

Yet Revelation 13, which depicts the persecuting Roman state as a many-headed monster and ally of the devil, should warn us not to misuse Romans 13. Its requirement of subservience to the state is neither universal nor absolute. Since we live in a democracy, we have a responsibility to speak out against injustice; uncritical loyalty is not a Christian stance. The duty of the state is not to oppress, but to prevent and control oppression, and to do so in a just and impartial way. A penal system in a democracy should be much more just than the arbitrariness of a dictator or the chaotic injustices of an anarchy. It can never be absolutely just (O'Donovan, 1977); but if it is consistent, proportionate and humane, it can claim to be *relatively* just. So justice without mercy is not just, rather justice and mercy are complementary.

The Christian who proclaims the good news cannot ignore its social dimension. Since Christ was the champion of the oppressed, his followers must show an active concern for the disadvantaged and be actively involved in seeking to change whatever structures of society permit or foster injustice (Sider, 1977). The good news concerns the coming of God's kingdom. I see no prisons there, and no distinction either between Jew and Gentile or slave and free. For God's kingdom is his rule of absolute justice and love. And until this is revealed in its final perfection, God's people are duty bound to demonstrate its partial arrival in their own lives and commend its ideals to society at large.

### (b) What should a Christian aim for?
God requires that we 'do what is just, show constant love and live in humble fellowship with him' (Micah 6:8). William Temple (1934) again helps us to apply our beliefs: 'But he [the offender] never is only criminal and nothing else . . . it is good to think more of what the man may become than of what he is. For in such a case the potentialities are actually greater than the actualities; and to treat the character as what it may be is to treat it as what in actuality it is; for it is chiefly potentiality'.

Jesus certainly tuned in to this potential when he spoke to his neighbour who was being crucified next to him. This is how the incident is recorded: 'The other one, however, rebuked him, saying "Don't you fear God? You received the same sentence as he did. Ours, however, is only right, because we are getting what we deserve for what we did; but he had done no wrong." And he said to Jesus, "Remember me, Jesus, when you come as king!" Jesus said to him, "I promise you that today you will be in paradise with me!"' (Luke 23:40–43).

Jesus did not use his power of freedom to come down from the cross, nor did he free this man from his cross. Far better, he promised him a place in his kingdom.

Our circumstances are not so extreme, and we have to search out our Master's way of tuning in to the needs of people – victims and prisoners and people generally. While Christian doctors and nurses concentrate on the needs of their patients, Christian teachers on the needs of their pupils, Christian social workers on the needs of their clients, we in the prison service must concentrate on the needs of our charges, though all within 'some reasonable measure of security'. The message of Martinson is not that *all* such efforts are futile!

Psychotherapy has also had to wrestle with the criticism that it did not do any good, for research has indicated that clients were overall no better for treatment. It has proved possible, however, to show that under the care of some psychotherapists clients improved at better than the average rate, while under others more deteriorated. It was possible to identify the 'good' psychotherapists and the qualities that made the difference. Three were distinguished:

1. Accurate empathy, or an ability to tune in correctly to what matters to the client.
2. Non-possessive warmth – which is a somewhat safer term than 'love'.
3. Personal integrity – or 'integratedness'.

A fourth quality seems to emerge from the literature, namely the confidence to hold the problem situation without being overwhelmed by it. A recent article (Sutton, 1979) describes this as 'persuasive power', but I feel this expression is not quite apt. I am indebted here to the work of Truax and those who worked with him. While it is not safe to generalize from this work, it is fair to make two points. First, Martinson accepts the greater success with a group of delinquents of psychotherapists who exhibit these qualities. Secondly, these qualities are most perfectly revealed in Jesus himself.

Roy Catchpole (1974) has described meeting a Christian who thus identified with his Lord. He describes movingly what a difficult borstal trainee he was, but goes on to tell how his chaplain ('as straight as a die') helped him to find Christ. Tony Grestone (1973) recounts a similar story, though it was a curate who 'tuned into' his needs after his release from borstal. Both men tell vividly how God saw their potential and led Christians to point them to his kingdom.

*(c) Where is the Body of Christ?*
The ability to reach out to another person with empathy, warmth and integrity is obviously not confined to chaplains; there are many other Christians working in prison who make such relationships and share freely their experience of Jesus.

They read lessons in chapel services and join in the worship – while maintaining necessary supervision – and they meet people where they are, in cell, in association, in despair, in hope.

But for all this, I cannot say that we Christians really represent the body of Christ; in a sad way we seem more often dismembered, too often just individuals, not showing that fellowship in which 'there is no difference between Jews and Gentiles, between slaves and free-men, between men and women', between 'screws' and 'cons'. We have not seized the promise that we are 'all one in union with Christ Jesus' (Galatians 3:28). Yet if we fail here, we fail to demonstrate the kingdom of God. Some churches worship and have discussion with prisoners, but I have yet to see in England the warmth of fellowship described by Chuck Colson (Chapter VI, pp. 176–177). At the same time, another borstal house-master and I took a small group of trainees to Lee Abbey (a Christian community in Devon) many years ago, and as they joined with an undergraduate working party in work, fellowship and worship they were moved by the love of Christ they encountered, and some were transformed.

Beyond these concerns for the one-to-one relationship and the creation of a real Christian community in a particular setting, I believe that we should exert ourselves, in a political sense, collectively. Christians should be involved in seeking to effect such changes as would bring more humanity within prisons, and more hope to prisoners and to those discharged. The Report of the Church of England's Board of Social Responsibility (1977) is a valuable starting point, but really needs the addition of a list of recommendations for action. I am not aware of any collective Christian initiative in presenting material to the May Inquiry. The Crime, Law and Punishment group within the Shaftesbury Project has begun to fulfil such a role, but it is a somewhat lonely voice. The recently formed Prison Christian Fellowship is an encouraging fresh initiative.

In summary, it seems to me that this is God's will: that we should love him wholly and our neighbour as ourselves; that we should live as members of his kingdom, freed from sin, death and oppression; that we should not acquiesce complacently in prisons, since they are a consequence of human hard-heartedness and not God's primary plan; and that if we truly love our neighbour, we shall visit those in prison and welcome into the body of Christ by word and action all those who believe in him.

**Dilemmas, alternatives and reform**
Some dangerous things have been done in the pursuit of prison reform. Chuck Colson describes in Chapter VI (page 153) the model penitentiaries of Pennsylvania which built out contamination but caused inhuman sensory deprivation. One consequence of our English enthusiasm for treatment and training during the early part of this century was the building of new prisons on sites remote from families. George Bernard Shaw (1922) is not the only person to cast doubt on prison reform: 'If any person is addressing himself to the perusal of these dreadful books in the spirit of a philanthropist bent on reforming a necessary and beneficent public institution, I beg him to put it down and go about some other business. It is just such reformers who have in the past made the neglect, oppression, corruption and physical torture of the old common gaol the pretext for transforming it into that diabolical den of torment, mischief and damnation, the modern model prison. If, on the contrary, the reader comes to the books as a repentant sinner, let him read on.' While Shaw would have us face up to the *morality* of imprisonment, it is primarily the cost that is compelling us to examine both penal reform and prison reform now. The two should be distinguished, for penal reform might take pressure off the prisons to allow reform there. A number of questions need to be addressed in turn, namely:

    a.  How are offenders dealt with now?
    b.  Who are the prisoners?
    c.  Can we abolish prisons altogether?
    d.  If not, how can we reduce the prison population?
    e.  Are the negatives of imprisonment reducible?
    f.  Can one set out a more positive regime in which Christians can play a significant part?

This will allow me to offer a personal conclusion stemming from the Christian perspective which I have elaborated above.

*(a) How are offenders dealt with now?*
Most offenders go free! The police detection rates for indictable (more serious) offences reported to them in 1977 stood at

forty-one percent. Zander (1979) has deduced from a sample of cases tried at the Old Bailey that the police are primarily successful 'where an accused is identifiable from the outset, where the public are co-operative in coming forward as witnesses, and where the offenders co-operate by providing confessions'! A large number of offences remain 'uncleared up' by the police and, of course, a far larger number are never even reported, leaving yet more 'offenders' at liberty (Farrington, 1973).

At the opposite extreme, in 1977 seventeen percent of the 180,923 males over twenty-one found guilty of indictable offences in England and Wales went immediately to prison. The remaining eighty-three percent were dealt with non-custodially. The distribution of sentences was as follows:

| Sentence imposed | Percentage of males over 21 dealt with | Change in the pattern of use of the sentence |
| --- | --- | --- |
| Absolute or Conditional Discharge | 9% | Steady |
| Probation order | 5% | Falling steadily |
| Fine | 53% | Fluctuating but about average |
| Community Service Order | 2% | Still in infancy |
| Suspended imprisonment | 12% | Steady |
| Immediate imprisonment | 17% | Steady |
| Otherwise dealt with | 1% | Steady (would include hospital orders, some of which would be custodial). |

(Table 6.3 of the Criminal Statistics for 1977)

This table does not indicate how non-indictable or motoring offences were dealt with: fines are imposed in over ninety percent of such cases. Cautioning of offenders (mainly those under twenty-one) without a court appearance is also not shown – this has increased markedly during the 1970s.[3]

In 1977, 40,021 males were sentenced to imprisonment: forty-three percent came from magistrates' courts (with sentences normally of six months or less) and fifty-seven percent from Crown Courts. This is a very sizeable number and would presumably have been higher but for the restrictions on the use of imprisonment and the alternative sentences which have been specifically introduced. Of these both suspended prison sentences and Community Service Orders (C.S.Os.) have become disposals in their own right and are now used in cases where a prison sentence would not necessarily have been imposed. In recent research Pease (1977) has indicated that about half those subject to C.S.Os. would otherwise have gone to prison. Some limited progress has been made in the provision of hostels, homes, day centres and detoxification centres for alcoholics, which the courts can use as alternatives to prison. But there are too few of them so far to make an obvious impact. Prisons received 40,000 men to serve sentences of imprisonment in 1977, without taking into account the many received into custody, as yet untried or unsentenced, or the women.

*(b) Who are the prisoners?*

There have now been several surveys of the populations of English prisons.[4] One such survey of a ten percent sample of the South East region's prisoners[5] sought to establish some basic facts about the main body of adult prisoners (Banks, 1978). The researchers looked at criminality, established criteria of seriousness and found that one third were petty or minor offenders. They studied the mental state of the population and found only a third 'normal'; twenty-one percent were recorded as having a gross or severe mental disorder, and the large remainder included the doubtful cases, the withdrawn and the institutionalized. The petty offenders tended to have disorders connected with drink, drugs, epilepsy or mental retardation, but the highest percentage of mental disorder was found among those with serious offences of violence against the person. They examined social factors and found that a third were homeless, three-quarters left school at the earliest possible date, that fewer were married than in the average population and that unskilled employment was most frequent.

The group of offenders which was categorized by the research team as 'petty' was in no way dangerous: most had poor work records, thirty-seven percent were homeless and ninety-four percent had got less than a thousand pounds from all their offences combined. This group were considered suitable for a non-custodial disposal without straining public tolerance. They look like the 'stage army' of homeless 'repeaters' who come to prison frequently and swell the figures of those received into prisons, but account for a relatively small proportion of the population. In their case courts have run out of disposals, for they have all been tried before, and prison is seen as a place of asylum. In prison their regular appearances lead to Christian name relationships and standard jobs; Fred would plant his seeds on one sentence and prick them out on the next. The postscript to the research report indicates that since the date of the survey (1972) this group has diminished in prison and the proportion of serious offences and longer sentences has increased. The 'stage army' is still with us, but at least more alternatives are being attempted.

Little is said in the studies about the social class of the prison population. This issue is not as simple as graffiti on the wall of Oxford Prison once suggested; one night there appeared mysteriously – outside – the question, 'Why are ninety-five percent of prisoners working class?' This was quickly expunged, but the answer rapidly appeared on the clean space, 'Because the working class commits ninety-five percent of the crime'. Many research studies have indicated that offending is not significantly class-related, but that offenders who are dealt with by criminal justice agencies do come predominantly from the 'working class'.[6]

We tend to deny that we have any political offenders in Britain. We have seen internment briefly, but we imprison those who challenge order only for their specific breaches of the peace. Their threat is presently recognized by their security category. Since the Mountbatten Report of 1966 prisoners have been categorized as A, B, C or D; category D men are classed as safe for open prison conditions, while at the other extreme category A men present a very serious risk. In mid-1977 there were 257 category A men. Category B men require a high degree of security to protect the public, and Category C men present less risk, both by the nature of their offending and by their propensity to escape.[7]

*(c) Can we abolish prisons altogether?*
The description of Categories A and B seems to deny a 'yes' answer to this question. But there are those who argue that institutions are altogether bad, or that they create the problems they appear to contain and so should be abolished. Massachusetts has seen the boldest experiment in this direction, in the closing of *youth* institutions by Jerome Miller in 1971–2. A network of community projects has taken the place

of state institutions; most projects are privately developed and places are 'bought' by the Department and are monitored by it. It is not a cheap alternative, but Massachusetts has avoided the greater costs of further institutionalization. The scheme has yet to be judged on the criteria of recidivism, the effects on the participants and public safety.[8]

A small proportion of those in custody in this country (especially in security categories A and B) are dangerous. I cannot therefore see that we can say we will have no imprisonment at all; such a decision would be no service to the community or to the particular offenders. Some will be in hospital secure units, some in prison.[9] Dangerousness has become an issue because longer sentences for 'dangerous' offenders may be the price which is paid for introducing shorter sentences for others. Professor Walker of the Cambridge Institute of Criminology has examined the case for longer prison terms for the dangerous offender. He has shown that while a man convicted of a dangerous offence is unlikely to offend in the same way again, he is more likely to do so than another man who has not previously committed a dangerous offence.[10] So, he argues, there is some justification for keeping three 'dangerous' offenders in some form of custody (subject to certain provisos) even if only one were likely to repeat the offence if released. Such decisions must be open to frequent review to prevent incarceration of unwarranted length.

Personally, I would conclude that some form of incarceration will be retained, that imprisonment cannot be abolished, and that we should prefer it, with all its imperfections, inhumanities and degradation, to either anarchy or to whatever controls drugs or electrodes might make available. We are only five years from 1984.

*(d) How can we reduce the prison population?*
As indicated above, many new forms of sentence have been introduced to save offenders going to prison – probation, suspended and deferred sentences, day centres and community service orders. Parole, too, results in many prisoners completing their sentences in the community. Some will feel, perhaps, that enough 'chances' are already given and that more might put the system of justice in jeopardy. But it must be said that other countries – Holland, for example – have far fewer people in prison than we have (Tulkens, 1979),

without greater recidivism. And it must be added that keeping 42,000 in prison is very expensive and will become much more so because of the cost of replacing decaying buildings and maintaining a labour-intensive service. To have fewer men 'inside' will be expensive; to have more men inside will be prohibitively expensive, or so I believe. As it is, we need more alternatives to prison; if the crime rate were to rise again, the quest would become yet more urgent.

I want now to consider briefly some of the alternatives to prison, which could reduce the prison population and indeed the numbers appearing before the courts at all. (Chuck Colson has also discussed this topic from an American viewpoint – see Chapter VI, pages 162–165.)

*i.* 'Target-hardening'. If it is made more difficult to commit crime, fewer offences will be committed and fewer prison places will be needed. There is a convincing case for reducing opportunities for crime by making telephones more vandal-proof, windows more secure, cars more immobilizable and goods further out of reach.[11] Construction may be more expensive and trade might diminish, but that should not stop the ideas from being put into effect.

*ii.* 'Decriminalization'. The number of acts that have to be dealt with under the criminal law might be reduced. In some countries shoplifting is no longer an offence. It would be humane to find an alternative haven for drunks, even if they have to be called 'detoxification centres' and funded by another Department.

*iii.* 'Diversion'. Different methods of dealing with identified offenders informally, with no appearance in court, could be explored. Police cautioning and liaison schemes are established examples in this country, and more elaborate processes have been developed elsewhere. The aim is to divert offenders from court appearances, from a reinforcing of their anti-social tendencies and so from future offending. Bob Holman has already alluded to the reasons for avoiding the public labelling which a court appearance inevitably brings (see Chapter IV, page 103).

*iv.* More parole or more remission. Virtually all prisoners serving more than a month are credited with one-third remission of the sentence, which can be forfeited for serious offences in prison. Increasing this to half remission has been suggested, but only implemented for adults, I believe, in Northern Ireland – where the remaining portion has to be served upon reconviction before expiry of the sentence. Such tinkering with remission seems unconvincing to judges and the general public, though I have not yet seen any results from Northern Ireland.

Parole can be applied for by prisoners serving twenty-one months or more, and fifty-nine percent of those eligible were released on licence in 1978; they are said to complete their sentences in the community. Parolees who reoffend or break the terms of their licence can be recalled to prison and often are.[12] As the public has confidence in the parole scheme, as the risk of reoffending within the licence period is not great, and as supervision during the first six months does appear to reduce the risk of breakdown, there may be room for extending a modified parole scheme for prisoners serving shorter sentences. At present the probation service is unable to expand to meet such a major commitment, and it is doubtful about the control element which increases the policeman's part of the probation officer's role.

*v.* Partially suspended, partially served prison sentences. A further development of the suspended sentence was included in the Criminal Law Act 1977 (s.47). This has yet to be implemented, but will allow courts to sentence to immediate imprisonment for a brief term while suspending the remainder of the sentence. I fear, however, that it would result in an increase in the number sent to prison, rather than enabling us to reduce the prison population as we need to.

*vi.* Shorter sentences. Some countries, notably Holland, manage their penal system with shorter sentences, and the Advisory Council on the Penal System has advocated shorter maximum sentences for the majority of offences.[13] This modest, cautious proposal did not get a good reception, for its publication coincided with a time when the 'law 'n' order' flag was being flown from many masts. A further criticism of the report was its proposal of an exceptional sentence for the dangerous offender. As we have seen above, we have to wrestle with this if it is the price of shorter sentences. Many lawyers and criminologists advocate shorter sentences without parole and without remission. This may or may not make sentences longer or shorter, but while it would make them simpler, we would lose a degree of 'leverage' on the offender both in prison and in the community. It does seem that the danger of recidivism is not increased by shorter sentences. Rather those who will offend can do so sooner – to the consternation of the victims and the police (Tarling, 1977). I would like to think that a reduction in numbers and a simplifying of procedures would allow prison staff to do some more effective work, preparing their charges for a more successful re-entry into the community. But I would be unable to guarantee this!

*vii.* More use of probation. Fewer probation orders have been made in recent years, in both numbers and proportion. While research has not shown intensive probation to be more effective, I believe there is scope for innovation and expansion of short-term work, matching officers and clients, etc.

*viii.* Extending the use of fines. Fines do appear to be an effective sanction for many offenders. But those fined must be able to pay, and must probably belong to a group whose controls will be reinforced by this means. Nevertheless, many prisoners serve short terms for non-payment of fines – one I remember served thirty days for failing to return his library books! Uncollected fines are a major problem; so it is difficult to envisage an increased use of fines as a means to reduce the number imprisoned, because those who go to prison are likely also to be bad payers.[14]

*ix.* A general amnesty. I read recently of the results of the general amnesty in Israel in 1967 (Sebba, 1979). Would you expect prisoners to respond to such generosity with abstinence from crime or with a wry smile? In fact it seems that recidivism rates were again much as before. However, prison overcrowding in this country is reaching such a level that we may have to consider a partial amnesty to relieve its worst effects. The question of whom to release comes later!

These and other means might be used to reduce the prison population and then to keep it at a lower level. Essentially we must answer the question whether we are to spend more on prisons or tolerate more offenders and more control – attenuated control – in the community.

*(e) Are the 'negatives' of imprisonment reducible?*
Chuck Colson has described from his own experience as an 'insider' the degradation of the prisoner from the moment he is received, stripped and scrubbed, to the helpless moment when he is still waiting for discharge to become a reality (Chapter VI, p. 155f.). He has vividly portrayed the almost inevitably evil and destructive nature of penal institutions (p. 158f.).[15] The more 'total' the institution, the more absolute the power, the more helpless the inmate (Goffman, 1961). Is it any wonder that offenders in prisons create their own 'sub-culture'? There is no escape for the offender whose pattern of short-term thinking makes the inmate power structure all important for survival; Polsky (1962) described vividly how delinquent mores were reinforced by gesture, threat and force. Isolation from the community removes the presence of guilt to a large degree, and replaces it with an antagonistic feeling ('Look what they're doing to me'), a feeling shared by those already in the institution (Fiedler and Bass, 1959).

Prison is often described as a jungle: can clearings be made and maintained? To begin at a basic level, we need to press for the removal of degradation. In English prisons we do not in fact scrub down the newly arrived prisoner (see Chapter VI, p. 155), though we do insist on a bath or a shower. Clothing does not always fit first time, but we can always do better the morning after. Yet for all the prison building and refurbishing, the overcrowding remains. Most cells are about fourteen feet by eight feet. In local prisons two or three men share that space, often for nearly the whole of the day. It is a dull, dispiriting existence, relieved by meals (which are now vastly improved) and by visits. But these are still infrequent – though we usually do better than the prescribed minimum of thirty minutes every twenty-eight days for a convicted adult. Prison conditions are depressing, more depressing for those who are already depressed by the loss of freedom, family and all the known connections with outside. Depression must be countered by active, realistic hope, by restoring to the prisoner the status he has lost, or better, by not taking it away in the first place.

Traditionally, convicted 'felons' became non-persons – their persons and property were forfeited to the Crown.

Gradually we have restored 'rights' to convicted prisoners, though they still cannot vote. Prisoners are not without rights; they have a right to see the governor, the medical officer, the Board of Visitors and the visiting representative of the Secretary of State. They can petition the Secretary of State, they can write to their Member of Parliament and they can have cases taken to the 'Ombudsman'. They can consult a solicitor and take legal action – even against the Prison Department, provided that they have first tried to achieve their ends within the system. Many of these changes have had to be won, and the European Commission of Human Rights – to which prisoners may address petitions without restriction – has had a powerful mitigating effect upon imprisonment (Zellick, 1974). While the issue of rights has been well aired in recent years, citizens cannot sue for statutory rights in the courts, and prisoners are not in a different position.

While a prisoner may see the governor or a member of the Board of Visitors, the criticism is often made that he cannot see someone independent. The Jellicoe Report (1975) advocated that prisons should have independent councils which would have no disciplinary function. There have also been calls for an independent inspectorate. Boards of Visitors are appointed by the Secretary of State, but are expected to be representatives of the public, concerned with the good running of the establishment and the proper treatment of prisoners (Cohen, 1976). While independence is a virtue if it means a fair and impartial determination of an issue, it is a vice if it destroys the accountability of the Governor to the Secretary of State, and of the Secretary of State to Parliament. If justice must not only be done but be seen to be done, the same is true of the exercise of accountability.

There is pressure for a number of other changes – including legal representation for adjudications within the prison, participation in management (Ward, 1972), and the right to conjugal visits. Such suggestions usually call for more resources and for change which may be counterproductive. For example, a more legal approach can have the effect of causing staff to withdraw from relationships with prisoners, at the very time when engagement and involvement are urged upon them for treatment and security reasons (HMSO, 1977b). It is facile to assume, of course, that if all these changes were brought about, there would be no more tensions in prison. Power games would continue to be played, usually in a civilized way, but by no means always legitimately. Nevertheless, I am convinced that to make any institution work, there must be trust; reform consists, in part at least, in removing obstacles to that trust.

*(f) Towards a more positive role for prisons*
With such a catalogue of negative aspects to contend with, is there any hope for the prisoner or the English prisons? Shaw (1974) has demonstrated possibilities. So I offer a general statement and a particular suggestion.

*i.* Prison is a place for new learning. For all their negative aspects prisons do provide: asylum, a haven, a relief, a control where personal controls have broken down, a limit to harm and destructiveness; a safe area in which new roles and ways of relating can be tried and tested, so that they can be integrated and strengthened in time for the real test in the old world; a place where new skills can be learned, trade skills, survival skills (Fawcett, 1979 for example) or even an Open University degree.

Different types of learning can be encouraged, more focussed than trial and error, through the development of insight, through conditioning and through identification (Rapoport, 1962). Change is difficult for us all (Keith-Lucas, 1966) but we do identify with others and adopt their successful behaviours, consciously and unconsciously. Towle (1945) described this most significant process at work in juvenile offenders,[16] and it is less specialized than insight-work and conditioning. There is no shortage of good role models among staff who in such a labour-intensive setting constitute our key resource. The staff *can* make a significant contribution to changing attitudes and improving social skills and want to do so (Thomas, 1972). It is the routinization of processes, the exaggerated fear of loss of control, the vulnerability of staff and their fear of failure that can so easily render them impotent and the institution destructive. Staff need good support to make their positive contribution, and research with lay helpers confirms their 'good' potential (Truax and Wargo, 1966).

*ii.* The development of the 'local' prison. My second suggestion relates to changes in our current pattern of varieties of prison. At present there are three sorts of prison –

'local', 'training' and 'special'. We have one special prison which offers psychiatric treatment. Training prisons are of all security categories, and people are sent there to benefit from their training facilities, from the local prisons which service the courts of each area of the country. This pattern needs changing. When I was at Oxford Prison, it was the 'local' for most of the courts of Oxfordshire, Berkshire and Buckinghamshire; it was the most over-crowded 'local' in England and Wales – an average of 308 in space for 163 in 1977. In order to keep the numbers down to that level, we had to export men to training prisons as soon as possible after their cases were finished, and they were sent to prisons as far away as Avon, Somerset, Dorset and Devon. This separation of an offender from his family, friends, probation officer and others in his community reduces their effect on him, isolates him and reinforces the process of institutionalization. Change is needed to give local prisons a more significant role, keeping prisoners geographically close to their homes.[17]

At present the probation service does its best to ease the problems caused by the remoteness of training prisons by arranging transport for wives, families and friends. Proximity would allow probation officers and volunteers to develop more direct relationships which can continue beyond release. The work of prison visitors who befriend prisoners, but whose relationships are often broken by distance upon release, could be made more viable. Clergy, too, or their lay parish visitors, could maintain or begin direct relationships with their absent neighbours. The body of Christ then begins to have more obvious existence and meaning.

An additional possibility afforded by my proposal would be that of progressive home leave: one hour at first and progressively a little longer, provided that the previous leave was completed satisfactorily. It should be possible for a man to be released on leave late in his sentence, with the probation officer having a power of recall if breakdown threatened. We can, hopefully, give up the arguments about conjugal visits then, too!

This reorganization to make prisons more truly 'local' would have other advantages. The 'dead' time during which prisoners await trial or sentence, under often the most restrictive regime in any prison, could be put to better use (King and Morgan, 1976). Probation officers for example, could assess the viability of a non-custodial 'contract' as an alternative to a prison sentence – not as 'plea-bargaining' but as an honest collaborative effort to find a just and realistic alternative to a custodial sentence. Recent research by Holborn (1975) and Fowles (1978) indicates no automatic benefit from probation work in 'locals', but with the whole population I see great potential.

If we are to make the local prison work effectively in such ways, both before and after a sentence (where absolutely necessary!), we must create some space. In order to do this and to reduce the inhumanities and degradation of overcrowding, we may need to shorten sentences artificially, either by increasing remission to half or by a partial amnesty. My preference would be for an amnesty, say with everyone being released a month early for every year left to serve. In the longer term we need to shorten sentences, and might abolish remission and parole as they now exist. The Dutch call anything over nine months *long* (Tulkens, 1979), while for us eighteen months is short. This might have a price, however. Reviewable sentences might have to be introduced for the 'dangerous' offender, within a maximum length decided by a judge, and more serious offences committed in prison would need referral to outside courts.

**Conclusion**
These are very simple outlines of the way in which we may be able to move forward beyond the current period of 'radical questioning'. I know that the solutions cannot be simple because the problems are not simple. Yet I believe that, by widening the possibilities of prison as a place of new learning and by developing the 'local' principle, we can achieve some changes which are both realistic and just, but which still provide adequate safeguards and security. In common with the other contributors to this book, I would argue that changes which create alternatives to prison or which make prison itself more humane are only *part* of the answer. They can make for a greater hope and lessen the destructiveness of institutions for offenders and staff alike. Ultimately, however, there can be no substitute for Christian conversion, for the kind of radical personal transformation experienced by Roy Catchpole (1974; see p. 130 above). So, while prisons are not God's primary wish, it is vital for Christians to

be concerned for prisoners, to visit and befriend them, to share with them the knowledge and experience of the Christ who came to set us free, and to welcome them into the body of Christ – which no prison wall can divide.

# Notes and References

1 Histories of Reading and Bedford Prisons have been fully documented by Southerton (1975) and Stockdale (1977).

2 Cf. Chapter II, pp. 45–50 and 60–65.

3 Where the offender admitted his guilt of an indictable offence forty-seven percent of those between ten and seventeen were cautioned, twice the proportion of ten years before; cautioning for those over seventeen has remained a steady figure of about three percent (Table 5.4 Criminal Statistics for 1977).

4 See for example the books by Sparks (1971) who examined the population of Birmingham Prison, and Griffiths and Rundle (1976) that of a London Prison.

5 The survey dealt with the prison population on 2nd February 1972 excluding the unsentenced, the civil prisoners, the fine defaulters and those serving life sentences.

6 See for example Tittle et al. (1979) and Bennett (1979).

7 There were 1311 prisoners serving life sentences in 1977 and in a recent Parliamentary answer it was stated that 1030 persons were serving life sentences in England and Wales for murder.

8 Research on the first was promised in 1978, but I have seen no results yet. There have been suggestions that recidivism increased at first, but is now, overall, not significantly different from before 1972. Some offenders are kept in adult detention, and a few secure places have been provided, some public and some private, to cope with the most dangerous. But the level of provision is far lower than in 1971. The scheme enjoyed strong public support at its inception, but this has fluctuated since, and not all reflections are as optimistic as Rutherford's (1978) on which this note is based.

9 The problem of the mentally abnormal offender, and the relationships between hospitals and prison, are discussed in the Butler Committee report (HMSO, 1975).

10 Scott (1977) examined the problem of predicting which dangerous offender will re-offend when no objective test is reliable; he saw no alternative to accurate case study and involvement on a long-term basis.

11 See the work of Mayhew, Clark et al. (1976) on 'crime as opportunity'.

12 The length of time on parole has increased to thirteen months, and the failure rate during the licence period has reached around ten percent (see Nuttall, 1977 and the Parole Board's annual report), but this is generally accepted without serious criticism. Some prisoners criticize

parole on the grounds that they have to 'grovel' for it by good behaviour, and so see it as a tool of suppression. But most criticism comes from lawyers and criminologists who fear the use of too much executive discretion and see in it effectively a second sentencing process (e.g. Thomas, ed. 1974). It is considered unjust – to oversimplify – because the better bets get both shorter sentences and more parole. This is probably a fair criticism, and Nuttall (1977), who studied men eligible and released between 1968 and 1970, found no significant difference in rates of re-offending between those who were paroled and those who were not. Later figures from those discharged in 1973 indicated a better than expected response by those paroled for longer periods – this may be a selection effect or may reflect the parolees' better home and job arrangements (Prison Statistics, 1977).

13 In *Sentences of Imprisonment: A Review of Maximum Penalties*, (HMSO, 1978).

14 Wilkins (1979) has produced a useful study of fine defaulters in Birmingham Prison.

15 Jessica Mitford (1977) has produced a highly critical review of American prisons: we should neither dismiss her observations as relating solely to America nor assume that every practice she describes is universal.

16 Charlotte Towle wrote: 'As the delinquent is thus understood and encouraged, he may come to feel different about authority and he may move into identification with the worker's attitudes towards social restrictions, gradually making them his own, apart from the worker. This will occur when the individual has considerable capacity for relationship . . . The juvenile offender . . . may experience through imposed authority more lasting ability to inhibit his unsocial impulses, providing conformity and consideration for others give him new patterns for relating to others which are more gratifying than the old ones.'

17 The previous administration accepted in its Green Paper *Youth Custody and Supervision; a New Sentence* (HMSO, 1978) this neighbourhood principle for offenders under twenty-one. The Howard League publication *Losing Touch* (King, 1979) makes the point that this argument applies to all prisoners.

# Bibliography

Adams, S. (1970), The PICO Project, reprinted in Johnson, N. B. *et al.* (ed.) *The Sociology of Punishment and Correction* (2nd Edition) (Wiley, New York).

Banks, C. *et al.* (1978), A survey of the South East Prison Population, *HO Research Bulletin*, 5, 12–24.

Banks, C. and Fairhead, S. (1976), *The Petty Short Term Prisoner* (Barry Rose, Chichester).

Barton, R. (1966), *Institutional Neurosis* (2nd Ed.) (John Wright & Sons, Bristol).

Bean, P. (1978), Alternatives to Rehabilitation, *Prison Service Journal*, No. 32, pp. 1–3.

Bennett, T. (1979), The Social Distribution of Criminal Labels, *B. J. Crim* 19, 2, 134–145.

Board of Social Responsibility (1977), *Prisons and Prisoners in England Today* (CIO Publishing).

Brody, S. R. (1976), *The Effectiveness of Sentencing*, HORU Study No. 35, HMSO.

Brown, M. (1969), Article in *Federal Probation*, June 1969.

Catchpole, R. (1974), *Key to Freedom* (Lutterworth).

Cohen, N. P. (1976), The English Board of Visitors, *Federal Probation*, Dec. 76, pp. 24–27.

Farrington, D. P. (1973), Self Reports of Deviant Behaviour: Predictive or Stable? *J. Crim. Law and Crimin.*, 64, 1, 99–110.

Fawcett, B., Ingham, E., McKeever, M. and Williams, S. (1979), Social Skills Group for Young Prisoners, *Social Work Today*, 10, 47, 16–18.

Fiedler, F. E. and Bass (1959), *Delinquency, Confinement and Interpersonal Perception,* Technical Report No. 6, Group Effectiveness Research Laboratory, University of Illinois, quoted in Cressey, D. R. (1961) The Prison: Studies in Institutional Organization and Change.

Fowles, A. J. (1978), *Prison Welfare*, Home Office Research Study 45, HMSO.

Fox, L. W. (1952), *The English Prison and Borstal Systems* (RKP).

Goffman, E. (1961), *Asylums* (Harmondsworth, Penguin).

Grestone, T. (1973), *They Put Me Away* (Scripture Union).

Griffiths, A. W. and Rundle, A. T. (1976), A Survey of Male Prisoners – some aspects of family background. *B. J. Crim.*, 16, 4, 352–366.

Hassall, T. (1971), *Oxford Castle*, Oxfordshire Prisoners' Aid Society.

HMSO (1978), *Criminal Statistics, England and Wales* 1977.

HMSO (1977a), *Prisons and the Prisoner.*

HMSO (1977b), *Report of an Inquiry by the Chief Inspector of the Prison Service into the causes and circumstances of the events at HM Prison, Hull, during the period 31st August – 3 September, 1976 (The Fowler Report).*

HMSO (1975), Report of the Committee on Mentally Abnormal Offenders (Cmnd. 6244) (Butler Report).

HMSO (1895), *Report of the Departmental Committee on Prisons* (Gladstone Report) Cmnd. 7703.

HMSO (1978), *Sentences of Imprisonment: A Review of Maximum Penalties* (ACPS Report).

HMSO (1978), *Youth Custody and Supervision – A New Sentence.*

Holborn, J. (1975), Casework with Short-term Prisoners, in *Some Male Offenders' Problems*, Home Office Research Study 38, HMSO.

Hood, R. (1965), *Borstal Re-assessed* (Heinemann, London).

Howard, J. (1777), *The State of the Prisons in England and Wales* (Warrington).

Jellicoe, Lord (1975), *Boards of Visitors of Penal Institutions* (Barry Rose, Chichester and London).

Keith-Lucas, A. (1966), The Art and Science of Helping, *Case Conference* 13, 5, 154–161.

King, R. D. (1979), *Losing Touch* (Howard League).

King, R. D. and Morgan, R. (1976), *A Taste of Prison* (Routledge).

Leach, E. (1968), *A Runaway World*, BBC Reith Lectures (OUP).

Martinson, R. (1974), What Works? Questions and Answers about Prison Reform, *The Public Interest*, 35, 22–54.

Mayhew, P., Clarke, R. V. G., Sturman, A. and Hough, J. M. (1976), *Crime as Opportunity*, Home Office Research Study 34, HMSO.

Mitford, J. (1974), *The American Prison Business* (Allen and Unwin).

Neale, K. (1978), Paper given at a Howard League meeting 4 April 1978.

Newton, M. (1971), *Reconviction After Treatment at Grendon* (unpublished) CP Report, Series B. No. 1.

Nuttall, C. P. (1977), *Parole in England and Wales*, Home Office Research Study 38, HMSO.

O'Donovan, O. (1977), *Measure for Measure: Justice in Punishment and the Sentence of Death* (Grove Books, Bramcote).
Pease, K., Billingham, S. and Earnshaw, I. (1977), *Community Service Assessed in 1976*, Home Office Research Study 39, HMSO.
Polsky, H. (1962), *Cottage Six* (Russell Sage, New York).
Rapoport, L. (1962) *The Dynamic Use of Ego Psychology in Education for Social Casework*, private paper delivered for NASW, Smith College Educational Forum, San Francisco.
Rutherford, A. (1978), *Decarceration of Young Offenders in Massachusetts* in Tutt, M. (ed.) q.v.
Scott, P. D. (1977), Assessing Dangerousness in Criminals, *Brit. J. Psychiat.*, 131, 127–142.
Sebba, L. (1979), Amnesty – A quasi-experiment, *B. J. Crim.*, 19, 1, 5–30.
Shaw, B. (1922), Preface to Webb, S. *English Prisons under Local Government*.
Shaw, M. J. (1974), *Social Work in Prison*, Home Office Research Study 22, HMSO.
Sider, R. J. (1977), *Evangelism, Salvation and Social Justice* (Grove Books, Bramcote).
Southerton, P. (1975), *The Story of a Prison* (Osprey, Reading).
Sparks, R. F. (1971), *Local Prisons: The Crisis in the English Penal System* (Heinemann).
Stockdale, E. (1977), *A Study of Bedford Prison 1660–1877* (London, Phillimore).
Sutton, C. (1979), Research in Psychology: Applications to Social Casework, *Social Work Today*, 5.6.1979, pp. 17–19.
Tarling, R. (1979), The 'Incapacitation' Effects of Imprisonment, *H O Research Unit Bulletin*, 7, 6–8.
Temple, W. (1934), *Ethics of Penal Action*, Clarke Hall Lecture No. 1 (Stanhope Press).
Temple, W. (1976 ed.), *Christianity and The Social Order* (SPCK, London).
Thomas, D. A. (1974), *Parole: Its Implications for the Criminal Justice and Penal Systems* (Institute of Criminology, Cambridge).
Thomas, J. E. (1972), *The English Prison Officer since 1850* (RKP, London).
Tittle, C. R., Villernez, W. and Smith, D. (1979), *Am. Soc. Rev.*, 33, 5, 643: précis in *New Society*, 12.4.1979, p. 90.
Towle, C. (1945), The Place of Social Casework in the Treatment of Delinquency, *Soc. Serv. Review*, 19, 2.
Truax, C. B. and Wargo, D. G. (1966), Psychotherapeutic encounters that change behaviour: For better or for worse. *Amer. J. Psychother.* 20, 499–520.

Truax, C. B., Fine, Moravec and Millis (1968), Effects of Therapist Persuasive Potency in Individual Psychotherapy, *J. Clin. Psychol.*

Tulkens, H. (1979), *Some Developments in Penal Policy and Practice in Holland* (NACRO) (Barry Rose, Chichester).

Tutt, N. (1978), *Alternative Strategies for Coping with Crime* (Blackwell and Robertson, Oxford and London).

Walker, N. (1978), Dangerous People, *International J. of Law and Psych.* 1, 37–50.

Ward, D. A. (1972), Inmate Rights and Prison Reform in Sweden and Denmark, *J. Crim. L. Crimin and Pol. Sci.* 63, 2, 240–255.

Warder, J. and Wilson, R. (1973), The British Borstal Training System, *J. Crim. Law and Criminology*, 64, 1, pp. 118–127.

Webb, S. and Webb, B. (1922), *English Prisons under Local Government* (Longmans, London).

Wilkins, G. (1979), *Making Them Pay* (NACRO).

Zander, M. (1979), The Investigation of Crime: A Study of Cases tried at the Old Bailey, *Crim. L. R.*, April 1979, pp. 203–219 (quoted in *New Society*, 10.6.1979, p. 583).

Zellick, G. (1974), Lawyers and Prisoners' Rights, *Legal Action Group Bulletin*, Aug. 1974.

I acknowledge my debt also to the Rev. A. Harvey for his address 'Custody, its Necessity or Otherwise' as given to the Prison Chaplains' Conference on 16th July 1974.

# VI Towards an understanding of imprisonment and rehabilitation

Charles Colson

## Introduction
In the first section of this chapter I want to consider the problems raised by the use of prisons from an American perspective, drawing in part on my own experience of prison. We will then review some alternatives to imprisoning offenders, before we look at some answers to the question 'Is the rehabilitation of offenders possible?' In particular, we will examine the impact and nature of Christian conversion. In conclusion, we will single out some practical ways of responding to the problems which we have identified in the course of the argument.

## Prison: an American perspective
The principal method of punishment employed in Western society, at least for the more serious offences, is imprisonment. The very fact that in public discussion, at least in America, the two terms – 'imprisonment' and 'punishment' – tend to be used interchangeably suggests how bankrupt our thinking is in this field. If somebody breaks the law, society says 'send him to prison'. Any punishment other than prison is met with a howl of protest because society believes the offender has escaped due punishment. Unfortunately, this is the way people have been conditioned to think.

Prisons are supposed to accomplish four things: first, to rehabilitate, secondly, to deter crime, thirdly to punish, and fourthly to 'warehouse' criminals (simply to keep them out of circulation). For the last two purposes, prisons do a relatively effective job. But let us consider the first two goals – rehabilitation and deterrence.

## Prisons and rehabilitation
There is a considerable degree of propriety in Christians discussing this particular topic because we were largely

responsible for establishing penitentiaries throughout the Western world. In 1790 a Quaker movement in Philadelphia turned the Walnut Street jail into the first penitentiary in America. The objective was compassionate. Instead of subjecting law-breakers to the inhumanity of corporal punishment, which offended the conscience of the Quaker, they placed them in a solitary cell where they could commune with God, and thus repent. The notion of a place for 'penitents' gave rise to the name 'penitentiary'. The experiment soon proved a failure. People left penitentiary, not having repented, but rather, having gone raving mad. The same is true of some who have to endure solitary confinement today. But after a few years, the public conscience had been eased by the belief that something humane and constructive was being done for convicts. A bureaucracy began to develop. The prison was there; so society might as well use it. In reality, nobody cared. The practice, largely unimproved, has continued to this day.

The building of penitentiaries has increased both in America and elsewhere. The penitentiary, as a primary method of punishment and rehabilitation, is a peculiarly American export. We should feel far more shame than we do.

In 1976 and 1977 a special Sub-committee on the Penitentiary System in Canada presented its *Report to Parliament*. A research staff travelled from coast to coast for seven months studying the Canadian prison system. In its exhaustive, well-documented report the Parliamentarians concluded:

> Society has spent millions of dollars over the years to create and maintain the proven failure of prisons. Incarceration has failed in its two essential purposes – correcting the offender and providing permanent protection to society. The recidivist rate of up to eighty percent is the evidence of both.[1]

The Canadian investigators' discovery is certainly not news to inmates. Gary Smith, a former inmate, made this telling comment during an interview on NBC's 'Today' show: 'You might as well say cologne cures gangrene as to say prisons rehabilitate people . . . prisons teach people how to do time. You can't socialize someone in prison.'[2]

The failure of our prisons is probably the only area where total agreement can be found between inmates and those responsible for the judicial and penal system. In a recent speech Chief Justice of the United States Supreme Court, Warren Burger, sounded like Gary Smith:

> We have developed systems of correction which do not correct . . . If anyone is tempted to regard humane prison reform as 'coddling' criminals, let him visit a prison and talk with inmates and staff. I have visited some of the best and some of the worst prisons and have never seen any signs of 'coddling', but I have seen the terrible results of the boredom and frustration of empty hours and a pointless existence.[3]

Many Quakers today realize that their forefathers made a serious mistake. The American Friends Service Committee's report on crime and punishment in America, included in an excellent recent publication entitled *Struggle for Justice*, concludes that 'suffering within the penal system has not decreased. The opposite seems to be the case: rehabilitation has introduced a new form of brutality, more subtle and elusive.'[4]

Seldom do liberals and conservatives agree on social issues. The failure of prisons, however, is one issue on which the Left and Right are united. For example, a very conservative Christian study group, the Chalcedon organization in California, says:

> Conservatives and churchmen who advocate 'stiffer' applications of the prison system had better reassess their efforts. They are demanding a humanistic plan of salvation. Biblical law requires restitution, not imprisonment.[5]

If prisons can bring together conservatives and liberals, and even captives and their captors, perhaps they have some redeeming social purposes after all!

The overwhelming weight of scholarly opinion also emphatically agrees that prisons simply do not work. Ronald Goldfarb, author of *Jails: The Ultimate Ghetto*, calls prisons the 'one billion dollar a year failure'. Actually, that assessment is much too low because law enforcement in the United States costs seventeen billion dollars per year. The direct cost of imprisonment in penitentiaries alone is over three billion dollars (not including capital investment and associated costs of courts, jails, probation, welfare for families, lawyers, to name but a few).

'As instruments of punishment, prisons have been a resounding success,' observes Charles E. Silberman, 'but they never have achieved their goal of rehabilitation. Over the last half-century, one crime commission after another has criticized prisons for their failure to rehabilitate inmates and has called for new approaches to achieve success . . . The Crime Commission's faith in the possibility of rehabilitation has given way to pessimism and doubt. The last ten years have seen a flood of scholarly literature documenting the failure of one approach after another.'[6]

The late Hans Mattick, the director of the University of Illinois's Center for Research in Criminal Justice, and a former deputy warden of the Cook County Jail, states: 'If men had deliberately set themselves the task of designing an institution that would systematically maladjust men, they would have invented the large, walled, maximum security prison.'[7]

It is time for our society to banish once and for all that superficially appealing, conscience-salving myth that prisons rehabilitate. They do not.

Anyone who has ever spent any time in a penitentiary will understand. How does one control a thousand men in a place designed to hold five or six hundred? This ratio of overcrowding in American prisons (and in some English prisons too), especially when they are run by overworked, undertrained, and often under-educated prison officials, results in the dehumanizing of the inmate population.

## My experience of prison

I well remember my own prison experience. When a person is brought into an institution, he or she is put into a hot shower and scrubbed down with a hard soap to get rid of the lice that are often carried from filthy local jails. All personal items are taken away. Giving up my college class ring to the officer who processed me would not normally have meant much, except for the fact that I wore it as a wedding ring. My watch, too, was taken from me. Family pictures and almost anything that would help preserve one's own identity are also removed. I was, like all other inmates, given a set of prison clothes. I was also given a grey, yellowish set of underwear that had five numbers stencilled on the front and stricken out. I knew that I was the sixth person wearing them. Ill-fitting brown dungarees with holes in the legs and black prison-made shoes were also issued.

Every penitentiary does the same thing. Only the standard colour varies. In the state of Texas, for instance, the inmates wear white because prison officials say that most Texas prisoners work in the open fields and white repels the heat. The prisoners, on the other hand, say it is because white makes them a better target if they should attempt an escape. Both opinions are probably correct.

I worked in the prison laundry. This ultimately allowed me to acquire brown dungarees which fitted properly. The indignity of prison clothing might seem a very small item to you, and compared to the other horrors of confinement it is. I do not dress any better when working in my garden today. But in prison it illustrates the intentional degrading of the inmate.

In some prisons, wardens ('governors' in English prisons) have relaxed the regulations, so that inmates can wear some items of personal clothing. In these prisons, simply in order to assert their identity, inmates wear the most garish kerchiefs around their necks. The sameness of the dress is but one factor in the regimentation and nerve-chaffing tedium of prison life.

One of the first things a prisoner learns is that he can make no decisions for himself. A bell goes off in the morning to tell him the day is beginning, and another goes off at night to tell him the day is over. In between, every decision is made for him: when and what to eat, what to wear, where to go, to whom to talk, what to listen to on the radio or see on television. The places to which he can and cannot walk are prescribed. Every day is identical to the one preceding it, and the same as the one that will follow.

Every hour or two there is a count; 'checks' they are called in English prisons. That word sends cold chills up the back of any inmate, present or past. It is the process by which men are required to return to their cells or their bunks, and then stand there while prison staff walk from bunk to bunk, cell to cell, conducting a physical count of all inmates. Since most institutions in America have prison populations of 500 to 2,000, the process is painfully time-consuming and often subject to human error. I remember the count taking from twenty minutes upwards, and continuing for several hours when someone is missing. When a count is taken at night the prison guards, most of whom find prison life as boring as the inmates, will often shine the lights directly in inmates' eyes. Sometimes the guards sadistically kick bunks as they walk by.

One of the things that gripped me, the moment I arrived in prison, was the sense of helplessness. Every prisoner experiences the horrifying realization that in order to be free, someone has to reach in from the outside and 'pluck' him out. It is an overwhelming sensation. I felt it the very first night in prison, lying in my bunk trying to sleep: the stale odours from the open urinals, the smoke filling the dormitory air, men getting up and down banging their lockers, cursing, the occasional violence (which is an everpresent reality of prison life), and the feeling of bitter despair that is so pervasive in every prison.

There are many paranoias which prisoners experience, like the feeling that walls are closing in or the staring at hands of a clock which seem never to move. I was with one thirty-eight-year-old inmate who had spent nineteen years – or half of life – in prison. He was used to it. He was institutionalized. He was told he would be released on the fifth of November. But when the day came, his papers had not arrived in the prison, so he was told he could not be released until the next day. That night he actually lost control of his senses, punched his hand through a wall, and had to be taken off to the hospital and physically restrained. One more day after half a lifetime might not seem much to some, but the fact is that this man was overwhelmed by the fear (experienced by many) that he would never get out of prison. Something would happen, he would die before being released, he would be forgotten, or the prison would lose his records. The feeling that 'They are playing with my mind' is a constant and universal complaint of prison inmates.

One prison counsellor told me that a chief reason for the high incidence of mental disturbance in prison is the inability of new inmates to face the horrifying reality of their plight. They simply escape into fantasies; 'spacing out' inmates call it. I have seen many men 'spaced out'. One at Maxwell Federal Prison, where I was imprisoned, was given no medical care for weeks until I threatened to write to governmental officials in Washington, D.C.

Many inmates try to cheat the government out of their sentence by simply sleeping their entire time away, and some are masters at it. Some inmates sleep up to eighteen or even twenty hours a day, and stay awake only long enough to eat their meals in the mess hall.

Some people compare prison life to the military. Having experienced both, I can say categorically that the comparison is a travesty of the armed services. In the military there is a sense of 'esprit de corps', a sense of purpose and usefulness; being in prison, on the other hand, is like falling into a dark, bottomless pit. In prison, I never heard men laughing in a good-natured way, seldom did I hear a joke told, and rarely did I see a genuine smile. Most conversations centre on the plight of the inmates. Complaining is the one therapy an inmate possesses. He thinks himself treated unfairly; he can pour out his troubles to another inmate who perceives himself as being unfairly treated as well.

The only military unit I can imagine which would even remotely compare to the situation inside a prison would be that of a submarine that has lost its power and gone to the bottom of the ocean, with very little chance of rescue.

The loneliness of prison life is aggravated by the fact that most families are unable to stand the strain of the 'bread-winner's' imprisonment. During my seven months of imprisonment, I talked to perhaps a hundred men who were undergoing severe marital problems. I have heard the figure, though I cannot vouch for its accuracy, that over fifty percent of all families break up after one year of a mate's imprisonment. From my experience, I think this estimate is probably low. It takes powerful marital bonds to survive extended imprisonment. The wife of a prisoner is often forced to work to supplement welfare. Visiting is difficult, both because of its cost and because of the restrictions of a penal institution. Conjugal visits have been experimented with, but only in some states and with mixed results. So inmates, naturally fearful of one another, experience few truly meaningful personal relationships at the very time when their outside relationships are being severed.

**Power and corruption in prison**
There are two other significant observations to make about prison life which bear upon an understanding of rehabilitation.

The first is that most institutions are run by the convicts. The prison staff make the rules, guard the outer security of the prison, and keep the public out, but order within the population itself is established by the inmates' own rather finely defined power structure. Lifting the heaviest weights, having the most violent record, and most flamboyantly defying authority are qualities which win respect and admiration from fellow convicts. The toughest convicts become the bosses.

Order is maintained by rigid systems of discipline. In America, for example, ten men were recently murdered, gangland style, inside the Atlanta penitentiary during a sixteen-month period. A governmental investigative report which I read contained two startling conclusions. First, every man died alone. No one helps anyone in the prison society, out of fear that he may be the next victim. That is part of the horrible loneliness and isolation with which every inmate learns to live. Secondly, the government investigators could not find the slightest clue as to who committed the crimes. The Atlanta penitentiary is an institution where two thousand men are packed together. It is impossible to find a nook or cranny safe from the view of others. Activities are monitored on closed circuit television, where the interior of cells can be seen through the bars. Yet ten men are murdered without a single witness! That surely says something about inmate discipline.

The second fact not commonly understood about prisons is that they harbour probably the most corrupt society anywhere. Prison officials have absolute power; the all-too-familiar maxim that 'absolute power corrupts absolutely' is nowhere more appropriately applied than in prisons.

The prison poison infects everyone within its reach. Narcotics are often smuggled in by guards, as well as by visitors and inmates. I was told of one guard in the prison in which I was held who, for a small fee, would bring in any brand of liquor any inmate wanted. Other guards were seen taking food out of the mess hall and loading it into their cars. No one would think of turning them in. It was something like a mutual non-aggression pact. Those same guards were known to look the other way when they saw inmates engaging in similar conduct.

The vast majority of prison staff are honest, decent men. But there is often enough corruption to infect the entire prison population. After all, how can an offender be encouraged to live a law-respecting life when he is confined in a pit of absolute lawlessness? He sees the law ignored or arbitrarily applied day after day after day.

I met one inmate, we'll call him Kirk, in one of our state

penitentiaries. Kirk happened to be a deeply committed Christian. One day he witnessed an inmate attacking another on the third tier of the cellblock. The man being assaulted shoved his arms forward, to deflect his attacker's thrust. The attacker tripped and fell over the guard rail to his death. The man who had been assaulted was charged with first-degree murder. By the inmate code, no one talks. Because the dead inmate has friends who will want vengeance, and the accused man also has friends, such incidents often touch off even more violence and additional killing.

But Kirk's conscience would not allow him to remain silent. He called the defendant's counsel and volunteered to testify. The day he returned from court, where the defendant was acquitted, prison officials notified Kirk that his parole, which had earlier been granted, had been rescinded. In this case, it was the state which retaliated against an inmate breaking the unwritten inmate code. The penalty was harsh. This man's decision to talk resulted in the addition of several years to his prison sentence. Small wonder the inmates obey the code.

The point is simply this: it should be obvious even to one who has never been in prison, that the life just described provides probably the worst imaginable environment in which a person who has broken the law or has a disposition towards criminal conduct could be placed, let alone rehabilitated.

It is, in fact, an utterly preposterous process: to put human beings in cages like zoo animals, strip them of their dignity and decision-making power, allow their families to disintegrate, subject them to such violence that most must carry a knife to survive, force them to live by a code where they never testify or tell the truth, submerge them in corruption of all kinds on all sides, force them to live in an atmosphere of bitter gloom where so many paranoias are nurtured. Then, after several years of such relentless torment, we shove them out of the front gate, usually with twenty-five dollars, a new suit of clothes and a bus ticket home, if there is a home any more. The guard at the front gate shouts, 'I'll see you in two weeks.' *This* is what society calls 'rehabilitation'.

To me, it is like throwing a hand grenade into a crowded movie theatre. It is sheer madness.

**Prisons and deterrence**
Prisons are supposed to deter crime. They do not. That is self-evident. For in America, four out of five crimes, whose

perpetrator is apprehended, are committed by ex-convicts. Depending on the state and the jurisdiction, the recidivism rate varies between fifty and eighty percent. In England, as in most of Europe, the recidivism rate is just as high. Some reports suggest it is even higher.

Then there is the illusion of a specific deterrent in prison, which is one reason society is so eager to imprison convicted criminals. For example, incarcerating a rapist certainly means that, while in prison, he is not going to rape anybody outside prison. Yet the chances are that he will rape someone inside prison. Nevertheless, free society, at least, is protected for the period of time the offender is confined.

Statistics provide some guide to the question whether crimes in general are being deterred by imprisonment. On the assumption that capital punishment is a severe penalty and hence a severe deterrent, homicide rates in various states of America where capital punishment is authorized can be contrasted with rates in states where it is not. Significantly, the homicide rates seem to be *higher* in those states which implement capital punishment than in those states which do not.*

I have interviewed several inmates on Death Row. Some are there because they committed a crime of passion, which means by definition that they did not think through the consequences of their actions. Neither prison nor capital punishment was a deterrent to them.

I also met a man who had killed twenty-seven people. He had been on narcotics. He went on a murder spree many years ago. He is still on Death Row in Idaho, waiting to be hanged whenever that state settles all the attendant legal issues. He had no idea he had committed the crime; he was in a deep narcotics trance, with no realization of what he was doing. So he was not deterred by the fear of capital punishment.

Another man whose case I have examined was on Death Row because he had been paid five thousand dollars to kill someone. The only thing the threat of capital punishment did for him was to raise the fee he charged to commit murder. The potential penalty was merely part of the overhead, a risk that he took into consideration only in monetary terms.

There has, in my opinion, been no valid demonstration that the existence of prison deters crime. This is particularly the case in America, where of every hundred crimes committed

* See Chapter II, pages 55–57 for a further discussion of capital punishment.

only two individuals are successfully apprehended, prosecuted and incarcerated. It is not the probability of imprisonment or even of capital punishment which deters crime, it is only the probability of being apprehended. Swift justice can do that.

## Some alternatives to prison

In concluding that prisons neither deter crime nor rehabilitate inmates, we are not without alternatives for dealing with offenders. These would be better both for society and for the offender. Some are proven and tested, and could be effectively employed immediately if only public and bureaucratic inertia could be overcome. They include the following:

### (a) Pre-trial diversion

Some jurisdictions in America provide what is called a 'second chance' system. A first offender or an unintentional lawbreaker is given counselling; if after a year his conduct is satisfactory, the indictment is expunged and his record cleared. This has proved particularly effective with youthful offenders. Additionally, studies have shown that the costs to the state are greatly reduced, and recidivism is also reduced dramatically. Much information is available about this promising programme which has been used with great success in New York State's 'Vera Project'. It is, however, a programme that has no constituency and, sadly, no public impetus behind it. Yet is is an important way to reduce the use of prisons.

### (b) Restitution

Making an offender repay his victim should be considered on a wide scale as a primary means of dealing with criminal behaviour. Restitution and compensation afford satisfaction to the victims of crime, instead of the abstract consolation that offenders somehow 'pay for their crimes' in prison. If restitution were adopted on a wide scale as society's primary postconviction response to criminal behaviour, there would be a far better rehabilitation of offenders than under the present system, and at an enormous reduction in cost. Christians should need little persuasion of the superiority of restitution, since it is biblically declared to be the prescribed response for one who has wronged another.[8]

In Kalamazoo, Michigan an experimental restitution programme has been conducted. Offenders have been required to pay back the victim of their crime or to pay into a criminal justice fund in the state. The resulting recidivism rate, among those so sentenced, has been cut to six percent. Similar success has been reported from projects in Baton Rouge, Louisiana, in Georgia, and in Lake County, Illinois.

## (c) Expanded probation

Some American prison officials believe that probation, at least with most non-violent offenders, is an effective alternative to imprisonment. With this concept, a convicted criminal loses part of his freedom but remains in the community. He is required to report each week to a probation officer who closely supervises his habits. His employment is monitored; reports are obtained from his work supervisor. His travel must be approved. His associations are closely observed.

Probation has the great advantages of keeping the offender's family intact, maintaining community ties, and requiring him to engage in responsible conduct by working for his own support. It is, in effect, a 'second chance' after conviction, though the stigma of conviction remains with all its attendant civil disabilities. Probation can also be used as a way of shortening prison sentences. Getting a man out of prison sooner, rather than later, will enhance the prospects of his rehabilitation.

The critical period of adjustment for an offender is the first ninety days of freedom. Often, someone returning home and to society from prison will experience great cultural shock. The sudden release of pressure and the new-found freedom create a trauma for which most prisoners are ill-prepared.

It is important for the offender and society alike to understand how difficult the re-entry into society can be. The world will not appear as the inmate had imagined it. All through his years of confinement he has fantasized about the glories of freedom outside a prison. In reality, he will be greeted by cold stares, he will have difficulty obtaining a job, in many states he will be unable to vote or hold a state licence, and he may have to register at the police station when visiting a new community. He will be socially shunned as if he were carrying a communicable disease. Even some members of his family and some of his old friends may reject him. At that point of despair, the ex-convict often decides that life inside the prison wasn't so bad after all. He has little to lose by returning to a life of crime.

The temptations are particularly great for offenders who have been dependent on alcohol or drugs; if they return to using them their freedom will be short-lived.

Sometimes the released offender, in his old environment, will find himself under incredible peer-pressure to re-enter a life of crime. I have talked to countless inmates who have expressed to me a deep-seated fear that when they return home, they will be coerced into their old ways.

Since these several factors make the period of immediate post-release adjustment critical for ex-offenders, the availability of probation and volunteer assistance is vitally important.

*(d) Community treatment and work release*
Many jurisdictions in America have experimented with the use of what is termed 'halfway houses' and 'treatment centres'.

In a typical halfway house, an offender lives in the facility but works each day in the community. Thus, his ties with society are not as violently ruptured as they would be in the case of imprisonment. He continues to be productive, yet his confinement for a portion of each day represents genuine punishment. Halfway houses tend to be smaller than prisons and provide more humane living conditions for their residents.

Another intermediate type of restoration of offenders to society is the community treatment centre. This is a small facility located in a community, as distinguished from the typical isolated, 'fortress-type' prison. In community centres, residents are given specialized treatment, particularly for alcohol or drug-dependency. And, since, as previously noted, a very high percentage of the American prison population is chemically dependent – one study shows eighty three percent – a community treatment centre offers the type of facilities that help the offender deal with the basic cause of his criminal conduct.

Such centres are far more effective for rehabilitation than prison, where a man's dignity can be so severely damaged that it is difficult to restore his self-esteem and make him concerned for his own rehabilitation. In fact, prison is by far the worst place even to attempt to rehabilitate an offender who is dependent upon drugs or alcohol.

## (e) Community Service

The great cry in America today is for punishment of white-collar offenders. Since punishment and imprisonment are synonymous terms to many, the clamour is for white-collar criminals to be sentenced to prison. This is the equivalent of saying that, since some people are wrongly executed, all people should be executed.

I operated a washing machine in the laundry at Maxwell Federal Prison. I had been told when I arrived in prison that I could not give legal assistance to other inmates. There were thinly veiled threats that I might be in trouble if I did. The prisoner operating the washing machine next to me was a prominent doctor who had been convicted of an offence unrelated to practising medicine. He had served on the Board of Directors of a local bank and had been prosecuted for a stock fraud. He was told that he could in no circumstances practise medicine. Now there was no resident doctor in this particular prison. Inmates' medical needs were provided by a paramedic. Meanwhile, my friend the doctor put dirty underwear into the washing machine each morning and took it out each afternoon. Coincidentally, there developed a shortage of doctors of his specialty in the surrounding area. As the end of his term approached, he volunteered to work evenings in a local hospital, but his offer was refused.

This tale is an illustration of short-sighted foolishness. Instead of being sent to prison, doctors, lawyers and others with professional skill could be required to work for a period of years, either at a very modest pay or none at all, in ghettoes, hospitals, or other areas of public need. Such alternative public service sentences need not be limited to white-collar offenders. For in every prison, there are skilled carpenters, plumbers, mechanics and machine-tool operators who could be assigned to community projects. Most talents could be constructively used for society's benefit rather than wasted, and even eroded through disuse in prison. The present system is indefensible. We could easily do better.

## The rehabilitation of offenders

### (a) Can offenders be rehabilitated?

To answer this central question, it is necessary to understand something basic about the nature of the men and women in our prisons. The prevailing public impression is that all criminals are violent. Some of them are even perceived as sub-human and innately evil, while the rest of us are innately good. The simple truth is that offenders cannot so easily be stereotyped. There is no such thing as the 'typical' criminal. He just does not exist. Instead, my own experience in prison convinces me that inmates are a diverse group of individuals who represent a cross-section of society, though comprising a somewhat higher percentage of the minority peoples and the poor. This is not because of poverty as such; it is rather because poor offenders simply do not have the adequate resources to defend themselves when tried in court. It is also because law enforcement agencies are much more aggressive in punishing street criminals than in punishing upper or middle class criminals.

In short, prisoners are fellow sinners and we all share with them a common heritage of sin. Bruce Jackson, a former inmate, explains it this way in his book *In the Life: Versions of the Criminal Experience*:

> We often read or talk about the *criminal* as if this were some homogeneous category, as if the word defined a personality type. It is no more useful than the word 'killer' which could, given the proper circumstances, cover any of us.[9]

Jesus Christ would not disagree with that observation. Offenders simply represent that part of any population which gets caught, as opposed to the many who are never apprehended. Remember that in the United States only *two* percent of all crimes result in the offender being apprehended, successfully prosecuted and sent to prison.

### (b) The problem of low self-esteem

In the course of training 1750 prisoners last year, we in Prison Fellowship* have discovered that they have one key fact in common: they are failures and losers at their 'profession'. This sense of failure commonly begins long before the criminal act occurs, as Gerald McHugh explains:

> Chances are that for most prisoners the experience of failure is not limited to his/her criminal career, the proverbial 'mistake' in an otherwise smooth life. On the

*For details, see the Editor's Note following Chapter I.

contrary, in the case of many if not most people in prison, being incarcerated is simply the most recent crisis in a lifetime of difficult situations.[10]

While I reject all easy stereotypes, we have found in our ministry that most offenders share a common characteristic of low self-esteem and excessive self-hate (see Chapter I, p. 31). Self-defeatism produces in them a negative self-image. Inmates often view themselves as 'born losers', a fact which drastically affects their opinion of others. Their constant feelings of rejection reinforce their disproportionate belief that we all live in a harsh, uncaring world in which everyone must fight for survival.

Understanding this compounding dilemma helps us also to understand certain patterns of criminal behaviour. For someone who has a very low opinion of himself or herself usually has an equally low opinion of other human beings. As a result, such people come to believe that to assault another is not to injure something of worth: to steal is instead simply to take something of worth from someone of no worth.

A person with such a low sense of self-esteem is gambling nothing in committing a crime, because if caught and sent to prison he has lost little of value. His life, he sorrowfully believes, is not worth keeping out of prison.

The prison experience, we have discovered, is the ultimate rejection for people who already feel worthless and rejected. In prison the inmate is intentionally made to feel totally worthless. The deliberate policy of dehumanization strips away the last vestiges of an inmate's dignity and self-respect. He is constantly reminded that he is a criminal. I remember a prisoner going to a counsellor with an urgent family problem: his wife was pregnant by another man. The counsellor sat back and, with a cold and unfeeling voice, said, 'Well, you should have thought of that possibility when you committed your crime.'

Everything about prison life drives the inmate deeper into his pit of self-rejection, thereby effectively conditioning him to commit further crimes.

In our Prison Fellowship ministry, we take teaching teams into prisons for a full week. During this period we emphasize the fact that every human being has been created in the image of God. We deal with the characteristics of God, stressing the point that God intends us to have his own characteristics. We further remind them that Jesus Christ, the Son of God, died on the cross for every human being – including those in prison. Perhaps Christ died even especially for those in prison. My reading of the New Testament leads me to conclude that Christ Jesus came to earth with a special burden on his heart for the poor, the disenfranchised, the sick, *and* the imprisoned.

Inmates hunger for the respect and love intended by God for his creatures. Members of the Observers Committee during the riots in Attica Prison, New York, noticed, for example, that inmates time and again emphasized their desire for respect. 'We will be treated as human beings,' shouted one. Another, near tears, swore, 'We will live like people or die like men.'[11]

Our first goal in Prison Fellowship through teaching and small group discussion is to plant in the individual's mind an awareness that he or she is of infinite worth in the sight of God. It is amazing to watch the transformation of attitude that occurs when this remarkable truth is understood, and believed.

Once this is accomplished, we attempt to take the inmate to the next step, which is personal repentance. This may sound like taking him to the top of a high building and then throwing him off. It is, rather, a necessary progression. For without genuine repentance there can be no genuine conversion. Admittedly, we must walk a fine line in our teaching between trying to develop qualities of self-esteem and at the same time leading people to repentance over the sinful nature of their life and conduct.

Both elements are absolutely essential to an inmate's understanding of the Christian message and true conversion.

*(c) Christian conversion*

I can tell you only what I have seen and heard, which is that men and women are genuinely coming to Christ, making a real commitment to him in their hearts, repenting of their past, and embracing the gospel. I believe in the classical Christian message of conversion, not only because of my own conversion, but because I have witnessed it in the lives of countless other prison inmates as well.

While imprisoned myself, I was part of a small prayer group which met regularly. Many nights, men would come to us seeking to salvage some meaning from their wrecked lives.

Some of the men were virtual corpses, with their bodies atrophying and souls corroding. But those who gave their lives to Christ I saw come alive, filled with purpose, meaning and hope. I have kept in touch with many of them. Most are out of prison now, back with their families, rebuilding their lives. And I am convinced that they will stay out of prison.

The term 'jailhouse religion' is common in America. It suggests that conversions experienced in prison are merely temporary and convenient poses designed to help an inmate with parole. This happens, of course, as it does for other reasons in every church. I have discovered, however, one reliable test for determining the sincerity of a Christian conversion. An inmate who continues to deny his crimes (although I acknowledge that some are innocent), to argue about his sinfulness and to protest the unfairness of his treatment may certainly be genuinely converted (for only God knows), but my guess is that he is not.

The true disciple of Christ is one who freely and openly confesses the wrongs of his past, is filled with repentance (though no longer with remorse) and is deeply grateful to God for delivering him from it. When he can accept all this and talk about it openly, he has been liberated from the past, from his sin and guilt. He is able to begin building a meaningful Christian life.

I do not wish to leave you with the impression that this process is either simple or unfailing or instantaneous. A person begins a new life with his conversion to Christ. But it is only the beginning. Like a baby taking his first steps, the new believer falters, stumbles and gets up again. It is not easy; indeed, it is hard.

Much of the so-called Christianity that is promulgated in America today falls into the category of what the German martyr Dietrich Bonhoeffer termed, in his book *The Cost of Discipleship*, 'cheap grace'. This is the notion that God will bless our lives and forgive us no matter what we do, and that the only thing required of us as Christians is to clap our hands and await the shower of Heaven's blessings. 'Cheap grace' is a one-way street, proposing to accept all God's promises with none of the attendant responsibilities in return. It is a gospel without the cross, without sacrifice, without commitment, and without death to self. It is a do-it-yourself god-kit, the ultimate device of ego-gratification in an egocentric era. This brand of 'Christianity', though I should not dignify it with the term, will not lead to the conversion of a prison inmate, any more than it will lead to the conversion of anyone outside prison.

The gospel we in Prison Fellowship preach and attempt to live is strong medicine indeed, radically changing the entire value structure of its disciples. It involves, as Bonhoeffer declared, a complete break with the past, 'for when Christ calls a man, he bids him come and die.'

The Christian, then, must adopt a new value system based upon the principles of the kingdom of God as revealed in the New Testament. Through the power of the Holy Spirit he is renewed in mind as well as in heart, and begins to see the world through new eyes. He views those around him with a new compassion and understanding. A genuine conversion to Christ demands a new lifestyle and new values. It is, in short, a radical experience.

This authentic Christian message and its subsequent experience brings about the reformation – indeed the transformation – of the most hardened criminals. As the Apostle Paul wrote, in words familiar to all Christians, 'I have been crucified with Christ. It is no longer I who live, but Christ lives in me.' (Galatians 2:20).

In some ways, prison inmates who have been stripped of everything in life, understand this fundamental concept better than those Christians who bask in the luxuries of an affluent modern society. In fact, I have encountered more deeply commited believers in prison than out of prison. I have also often found that the longer a man's sentence, the more intense his discipleship.

*(d) The impact of conversion*

There was, for example, the black inmate by the name of Sammy in the Atlanta penitentiary, where there has been so much killing (see p. 159). He came to a saving knowledge of Christ one night after I had preached there to some eight hundred prisoners. Sammy was serving a sentence of 'life plus fifty years'. The judge who sentenced him to prison wanted to be sure that Sammy never got out. So the transformation of Sammy was one of the most remarkable things I have ever seen. A tough, bitter and angry man was converted by the grace of God into a Christian always beaming with a radiant smile, though at that time he was still serving a prison sentence of life plus fifty years.

About three months after he had become a Christian Sammy wore a continual smile. 'How are things going?' I asked him then. 'Great,' he replied, explaining, 'Right after you were here, my sentence was cut from life-plus-fifty to straight life.'

Four months later I was in Atlanta again, and Sammy wore an even bigger smile. 'Sammy, what has happened?' I inquired. 'You won't believe this,' he responded, 'but the day after you were here to visit me the last time, it was cut from life to just fifty years,' he said of his prison term. Then, with the most hopeful expression I have ever seen, Sammy asked, 'When are you coming back again?'

Dr Samenow, who along with Dr Samuel Yochelson conducted the exhaustive and valuable study I discussed in the first chapter, (see pages 31–34) agrees that the first step necessary to reform an offender's behaviour is to change his value structure. During an interview on national television in 1977, he said:

> We found the task of change involved changing a man's thinking. It isn't just changing his environment. You don't change the inner man by changing the environment, and I think that social programmes have proved that. The task is much larger. It's to take a man's thinking and to identify the thinking errors and to offer correctives. It's – it's to change a man's entire view of life. [12]

What Dr Samenow said affirms the truth enunciated by Jesus that 'it is not what goes into a man that defiles him, but what comes out.' (Matthew 15:17–20). It is significant that after sixteen years of study, Dr Samenow and Dr Yochelson came to the same conclusion that the historic Christian faith has maintained for nearly two thousand years.

Men and women such as Sammy can become, by the grace of God, instruments for transforming the institutions in which they live. As a result of the ministry of Prison Fellowship, for example, the Atlanta penitentiary enjoyed twelve months of relative tranquility, after a rash of brutal killings.

The change at Atlanta was due to many things: security was tightened, some of the more dangerous inmates were transferred, improvements were made in staff, and new prison policies were instituted by the excellent warden. But the change was due as well to the fact that there are now three hundred inmates, out of a population of nearly two thousand, who are participating in chapel programmes. When we began our Prison Fellowship ministry there three years ago, only eight committed Christians were to be found. Now, by God's grace, there are three hundred.

These men in Atlanta truly live the gospel. There are prayer groups in virtually every cellblock. If someone is lying hurt on the ground, these Christian prisoners do not walk by him or leave him alone to die, as stipulated by the code behind the walls. Instead, they stop to help him. And there are other models of true Christian community in every area of that prison. For instance, fifty community volunteers regularly visit and work in the prison throughout the week.

It would be arrogant to assert that the influence of Christians is solely responsible for the change in the Atlanta prison, but it would be wrong to say that it has not been a major factor.

In prison after prison, we have seen similar pockets of spiritual transformation which have altered life within the institution. Evangelists have often been criticized for using the gospel to keep oppressed peoples in submission. But this is not the kind of impact that we seek. Rather, we believe we strengthen and embolden inmates and volunteers alike to stand firm on issues of human justice.

Those we are able to bring out of prison through Prison Fellowship to train for two weeks always visit prison officials, senators and congressmen. Each group of prisoners has talked about a lack of medical care, the need for better facilities and reformed procedures. Usually, I get a letter about a month later stating that, as a result of the inmates' effective presentation of their case in a Christian context, people have begun to see one another as human beings, rather than as numbers.

**What we can do**
What can be done about the problem of crime and punishment?

*(a) Changing the system*
First, we must band together to advocate sweeping changes in the way society tends to view the origins of crime and the proper nature of punishment.

Today, and for centuries past, prisons have been part of what sociologist Philip Slater calls 'The Toilet Assumption'. He writes:

> Our ideas about institutionalizing the aged, psychotic, retarded and infirm are based on a pattern of thought that we might call the Toilet Assumption – the notion that unwanted matter, unwanted difficulties, unwanted complexities and obstacles will disappear if they are removed from our immediate field of vision . . . Our approach to social problems is to decrease their visibility: out of sight, out of mind . . . The result of our social efforts has been to remove the underlying problems of our society farther and farther from daily experience and daily consciousness, and hence to decrease, in the mass of the population, the knowledge, skill, resources, and motivation necessary to deal with them. [13]

This is a chief reason why prisons in America are generally built in the most remote areas of the country. Even the socially conscious urban legislators vote to place prisons in rural regions. Just as we do not want to stare at an ugly sore on our bodies, so we put prisons and their ugly sores out of sight. But unfortunately, putting prisons out of sight also puts their residents out of reach of the community where the real solutions to prison problems are to be found. [14]

The Canadian Report, to which I referred earlier, correctly observes that one of the failures of the prison system is to encourage the idea that offenders can be removed from the community and made the responsibility of 'someone else'. The Report emphasizes the importance of community involvement in dealing with those who have broken society's laws:

> No penitentiary service can succeed without understanding and participation by the public. Prisons belong to the public, and therefore the people who pay for them have a vested interest in their remaining peaceful and in serving their best interests . . . The community also should participate and concern itself with the job the prisons are doing, if for no other reason than for its own safety. [15]

There is no point of greater importance for a basic understanding of the problems of crime and punishment.

An army of advocates is needed who can really begin to bring about change in our system. We need to reduce our prison population, not increase it. The Federal prison system in America last year reduced the inmate population by four thousand inmates simply by beginning to employ some of the constructive reforms we have considered. We need to expand compensation orders, probation and community service endeavours. We need to make use of halfway houses. We need to make prisons more humane and modern. We need to provide the financial resources necessary to care better for those we must confine.

We must decriminalize minor offences and look for pre-trial diversion programmes and opportunities. We must work for rational sentencing and parole. You need great changes in your parole system here in Britain as we do in America. Many states are adopting predeterminate sentencing. This avoids giving a prisoner the painful torture of not knowing either when he is going to get out or by what standards he has to behave in order to gain his parole or his release from prison.

Another area which would abate some public pressures for the incarceration of offenders would be compensation by criminals of the victims of their crimes. This is something desperately needed, not only as a service to criminals who can be rehabilitated, but to the innocent victims of crime.

Genuine reform will come only when the public is made far more aware of the causes of crime and of the alternatives to the imprisonment of offenders. The public also needs to be more aware of the terrible conditions of life in prison.

### (b) Helping the individual

Secondly, there is room for considerable development of voluntary one-to-one links between those inside and outside prison. The Prison Fellowship is one of several organizations which seek to match volunteers, person-to-person, with inmates. One visitor takes responsibility for helping one inmate, going to see him, corresponding with him, and helping him find a place to live and a job to do when he is released from prison. In certain areas, where this kind of programme has been developed, the recidivism rate has been cut from the typical seventy percent to below ten percent.

Our experiences in Prison Fellowship convince me that the faster more people become involved in caring for the men and women behind bars, the quicker will be resolved at least some of the problems of crime and punishment in our society. We simply cannot pass off the responsibility of care to someone else, particularly the duty to care for the men and women in our local prisons. Those who violate our laws must be punished, but they must also be encouraged to re-enter the life of our communities. If this is to be accomplished; we must have people caring for people, not merely more or bigger institutions.

A word of caution is in order; let us be realistic. A wonderful Christian friend of mine was recently working with an inmate in a Bible study group in a federal prison in Minnesota. The inmate was released and arrived on a Saturday morning at the doorstep of my friend's home. My friend was going away for the weekend, so he said, 'Here are the keys to my car. Here's a hundred dollars. Here are the keys to the house. Make yourself at home over the weekend. I'll see you Monday morning.'

Anyone who works with prisoners knows exactly what happened. The man ended up drunk with a girl in his arms and the car in the ditch. He didn't survive his freedom for twenty-four hours. The over-abundance of freedom he was granted was like giving an alcoholic a drink or giving matches to a child. Care must be exercised, but community concern for prisoners does work. There is, for example, a businessman in Iowa who has hired a hundred and fifty ex-convicts. He has yet to have his first problem. In fact, he describes the ex-offenders as his best workers. One reason why he has not had a problem is that he is willing to get up at six a.m., and go down to his plant and sit in his office. He tells his men, 'Between six and seven, you come and see me, I'm your brother. After seven a.m., I'm your boss, and every morning you can come and talk to me.' And every morning there's a stream of men who come in for that kind of help and counselling.

Helping ex-convicts, in this way, is not easy work. There is no simple way to do it. It takes patience, perseverance, love, and a willingness to extend to those who are thirsty a cup of cold water in the name of Christ.

## (c) Our Christian duty

Christians, of course, should not need to have their understanding increased or their consciences pricked in order to prompt them to go into prisons. Nor should they need to be motivated by good social arguments, because they have a very direct injunction to visit those in prison from the Lord Jesus Christ himself:

> I needed clothes and you clothed me, I was sick and you looked after me, I was in prison and you came to visit me.
> Then the righteous will answer him, 'Lord, when did we see you hungry and feed you, or thirsty and give you something to drink? When did we see you a stranger and invite you in, or needing clothes and clothe you? When did we see you sick or in prison and go to visit you?'
> The king will reply, 'I tell you the truth, whatever you did for one of the least of these brothers of mine, you did for me.' (Matthew 25:36–40).

I am sometimes accused of being a 'do-gooder', because of my concern for prisons and for the people who populate them. The simple fact is that I am not a do-gooder; I do not have any native good within me. I am simply coming to understand, in classical Christian terms, the nature and extent of my own sin.

Some people say that I go into the prisons because I have been taken in by the 'social gospel'. I know only one gospel, the gospel of Jesus Christ. I also believe in the truth of the Bible and in its authority for my life. Further, the biblical gospel has clear social implications, for Christ Jesus was as concerned with feeding the hungry as with proclaiming the Good News and forgiving sinners.

No, I go where I go, and I do what I do simply out of gratitude to God Almighty for what he has done in my life. Every Christian in obedience to Scripture belongs in those hard, tough places where people thirst and hunger, not only for food and drink, but for the more intangible – and the more important – foods of redemption and hope.

An experience in an American prison a few months ago brought forcefully home to me the tremendous differences which individuals can achieve when they begin to deal with the problems of crime and imprisonment. It happened during a visit to Colorado in the great, open spaces of America's West. One afternoon we flew in a small plane from Denver the capital of the state, due south to a remote community known as Canyon City. It is a lovely little town of twenty thousand people at the base of the Rocky Mountains. The principal reason for the town's existence is that one of the toughest prisons in America, a hundred-year-old fortress penitentiary, is located there. Behind its huge forbidding grey walls live two thousand inmates.

On our way to the prison chapel, I asked if I could visit Housing Unit 7, where so many severe problems had repeatedly occurred. The warden refused, and I could understand why when we heard the distant screams.

In that unit men are locked up, like animals in cages, for twenty-one of every twenty-four hours of the day. Many of them go raving mad. We did manage to walk through one housing unit, comprised of two cellblocks, five tiers high on either side. There was a steel grating overhead to keep garbage (and sometimes bodies hurled from the upper tiers) from reaching the concrete floor. On either side were rows of six-by-nine-foot cells containing men who stared out, their dead eyes following our every step.

That night, we assembled for a beautiful service in the prison chapel. But it was an event that took place as the service ended that I will never forget.

As the inmates were being marched out, one young man, perhaps in his mid-twenties and in appearance of Spanish ancestry – perhaps a Mexican-American – clutched at my arm. 'Mr Colson,' he said, 'there's something I must tell you. I have been in this place eight years. I have no family. No one has ever visited or called me, but six months ago I wrote to you, and you put me in touch with a family in Colorado Springs by the name of the Antonsens.' By now, tears were rolling down his cheeks, though the most radiant smile was on his face. He said to me, 'I just want you to know that for the first time in my life, I have hope and a reason for living.'

Think of it. One Christian who cared enough about another human being to give of himself, to share God's love, had enabled this young man to gain a reason for living. Of course he is a criminal. He probably did some terrible things. He may even be one of the most unlovable people in society. Yet he is a human being created by God with a life to be redeemed. It was *God's* love, manifested by that one family, that brought the message of redemption in Jesus Christ to him.

I don't even know that inmate's name. I don't know whether he will survive his time in prison. He has, I think, a long sentence to serve. I don't know whether he will make it if and when he does get out. But if he does, it will be because one Christian cared enough to extend a loving hand to another who was forgotten, despised, lost and rejected. And, simply put, that is the beginning of an answer to the problem of crime in our society.

It is no instant panacea. It will not always work. Some prisoners will appear to be rehabilitated only to fall away. Others will grievously disappoint us in other ways. But it is the one hope.

In the process of getting more people involved in prison reform, changes will inevitably occur in the structures of crime and punishment in our society. Christians belong in the front lines of the battle against injustice.

Maybe, if we are still and listen, we might hear echoing in the distance the words of the prophet Amos: 'Hate evil, love good; maintain justice in the courts. Perhaps the Lord God Almighty will have mercy on the remnant of Joseph. Let justice roll on like a river, and righteousness like a never-failing stream.' (Amos 5:15, 24).

# Notes and References

1 *Report to Parliament*, by the Sub-Committee on the Penitentiary System in Canada (Ottawa, 1977), p. 35.
2 Interview with Gary Smith, former inmate, on 'Today' show, NBC, January 17, 1974, quoted in Paul D. Schoonmaker, *The Prison Connection* (Valley Forge, 1978), p. 40.
3 Chief Justice Warren E. Burger, quoted in 'Prisons – Is There Any Hope?, *A. D. Magazine*, January 1973, quoted in Schoonmaker, p. 40.
4 *Struggle for Justice: A Report on Crime and Punishment in America*, American Friends Service Committee (New York, 1971), p. 96.
5 *The Chalcedon Report*, January, 1979, No. 161.
6 Charles E. Silberman, *Criminal Violence, Criminal Justice* (New York, 1978), p. 372–373.
7 Hans Mattick, as quoted in Hawkins, *The Prison*, quoted in Silberman, p. 382.
8 Exodus 22:1–4.
9 Bruce Jackson, *In the Life*, quoted in Gerald Austin McHugh, *Christian Faith and Criminal Justice* (New York, 1978), p. 181.
10 McHugh, p. 72.
11 McHugh, p. 81.
12 'The Criminal Mind', produced by Jim Jackson, *60 Minutes*, Vol. IX, No. 22, as broadcast over the CBS Television Network, Sunday, February 20, 1977.
13 Philip Slater, *The Pursuit of Loneliness*, Allen Lane, 1971, p. 15.
14 This issue is discussed in relation to the need for a change in the function of English 'local' prisons in Chapter V, pp. 142–144.
15 *Report to Parliament*, op. cit.

# Postscript

Nick Miller

After each of the six London Lectures had been delivered, there was the customary short period for questions. The somewhat formal setting in All Souls Church, Langham Place, and the considerable numbers of people present made it difficult to take full advantage of this opportunity. In addition, the fact that the six papers were given by five different lecturers over a six week period made the task of identifying common themes or of contrasting differing points of view well-nigh impossible. In this brief postscript to the book, therefore, I want to offer a personal reaction to the material which has been so painstakingly prepared and so lucidly presented, seeking to highlight for further reflection and discussion some of the key issues which have been raised.

These observations should not be taken to imply that any of the contributors failed in his brief. They are offered in the hope that they may help to link together the extensive material that has been produced, and they raise questions rather than attempting to answer them. In general my comment is restricted to areas which have been discussed in the foregoing chapters. Inevitably each author has made only a selection of the vital issues, and has been obliged to leave others unexplored.

## Some recurrent themes

### (a) Criminal justice and social justice

A central motif throughout the book is that crime and society's response to it are only part of a complex network of social issues, which raise fundamental questions about justice and community responsibility. Chuck Colson began his chapter by pointing out the problems of defining what 'crime' is[1] and he pointed out the interaction between crime and intractable social issues such as racism, poverty and materialism.[2] Commissioner McNee deals at length with the police role in maintaining civil order[3] and with the difficulties the police face as representatives of 'the state' in dealing with the disadvantaged, particularly among ethnic minority communities and young people.[4] Bob Holman has drawn out the effects of poverty, both in the real life of the families with whom he is in contact on his council estate[5] and in the research literature,[6] while Mike Jenkins summarizes research evidence revealing the frequent background of homelessness, mental illness and unemployment among many of those in our prisons.[7] This broadening of the focus from a consideration of crime and the criminal to wider social issues reminds us forcibly that the search for criminal justice is only part of a wider search for *social justice*: it is hardly likely that we will find a just and unimpeachable criminal justice system within the context of an unjust society.

Chuck Colson and Bob Holman have grappled with a range of alternative *explanations* for crime and delinquency[8]: there is a similar variety of ways of explaining the wider problems of our contemporary society. Equally, just as there is a broad range of different *responses* suggesting how we might seek to reduce the breaking of the law by offenders, so in relation to the bigger social problems we encounter many alternative remedies. The various explanations and remedies, which derive from the ideologies and the positions of power of those expressing them, frequently conflict with one another.[9] Consensus may seem increasingly hard to come by, though this is hardly a uniquely contemporary problem. There is historical evidence[10] of considerable conflict in the course of the development of current institutions of criminal justice (such as the police and the prisons), and in people's understanding of their relation to the problems of poverty and social control.

*(b) The responsibility of the individual – absolute or negligible?*
Placing crime in the context of wider social problems has been linked, perhaps particularly in the post-war period, to a 'liberal' belief that an individual's behaviour is largely determined by his circumstances, his background and so on.[11] This view has been widely challenged by Samenow and Yochelson, and by many others,[12] who lay a strong emphasis on the responsibility and freedom of the individual. The criminal justice system, with its individualistic core, finds it hard to deal

with a wider view, though there is a place for 'mitigation' in appropriate circumstances (for example, where an offender is unemployed or homeless). The various lecturers grappled with this central issue. At the end of a detailed and wide-ranging discussion in his first chapter, Chuck Colson stated his conclusion that the individual must be held 'ultimately responsible' for his actions: 'Crime is generally the result of a conscious and deliberate decision – . . . it is nonetheless nurtured by a complex root structure which reaches deep within the soil of our society.'[13] He gave examples of these roots, including racism, poverty and the ways social values are shaped by the media.[14] His overall conclusion seems to accord with the research evidence quoted by Bob Holman on why young people say they commit offences.[15] For the most part there appears to be a purposive element involved, including either material gain or boredom. These, however, may reflect conscious or unconscious feelings of economic disadvantage,[16] lack of access to leisure facilities, or significantly different 'norms' as to conduct which is deemed 'acceptable' and legitimate.[17]

Where the balance is assessed to lie between an individual's responsibility and the effect of wider social influences will have significant implications in determining what response should be made to the offender and to the offence. A strongly individualistic view will result, at its most stark, in the recruitment of more police, more court appearances and more stringent penalties. On the other hand, the focus on the wider social circumstances and their impact on individual decision-making will suggest a greater commitment to such responses as community development, initiatives in education and employment and seeking a more just income distribution.[18] These significantly divergent approaches (which may crudely be labelled a 'justice' approach and a 'welfare' approach respectively) are most obvious in English legislation relating to children who break the law and other children who need help,[19] but are also evident in the 'moralistic' and 'reductivist' approaches to sentencing.[20]

### (c) Controlling crime and dealing with offenders
The balance between the individual and the wider community is also reflected in the complex and often emotive debates on the limits on means of controlling crime and on how offenders are dealt with. This third theme recurs in the book. What

limits should be placed on police action in the investigation and prevention of crime?[21] What is the place of prisons, particularly in regard to dangerous offenders, and what rights should prisoners have?[22] How can we deal with offenders outside prison walls?[23] Is there a place for capital punishment or for corporal punishment?[24]

One thing is made abundantly clear both by Chuck Colson, with his own substantial experience of life and work in prisons, and by Mike Jenkins after twenty years' work in the English Prison Department.[25] Both stressed that there is little evidence of penal institutions being effective either in rehabilitating or in deterring offenders.[26] They demonstrate that the many negative aspects of 'sub-cultures' in institutions and the dehumanizing effects of their régimes are inevitably counter-productive to those ends.[27] This conviction leads them to a consideration of more hopeful means of dealing with offenders both within and outside the criminal justice process.[28] These may range from alternative non-custodial sentences to the commitment of Bob Holman and his colleague to work with young people on a council estate, seeking to prevent delinquency.[29]

The 'radical questioning' which pervades penal philosophy today may suggest that we might deal more effectively with the high levels of recorded crime[30] by increasing police manpower and widening police powers. This would indeed probably result in more formal control of public behaviour, while a possible increase in the capacity to detect crime might well deter some potential offenders. However, a likely outcome would also be that more offenders would be going through the criminal justice process. If this were to come about, and if prisons were *not* to be used in greater measure, the question would have to be asked how far the public are prepared to tolerate more attempts to punish and/or rehabilitate offenders in the community.[31] We find ourselves coming full circle to issues of community responsibility and the need for further attempts to prevent people coming into conflict with the law in the first place.

### The possibility of a Christian view?
The book rests on the implicit assumption that it is possible to formulate a Christian perspective on crime. Each contributor explicitly shares his understanding of the relationship between Christian faith and the issues he deals with. Thus

Christian approaches are suggested to such fundamental political and social questions as the place of the state,[32] the safeguarding of certain social values,[33] and personal commitment to individuals in trouble.[34] I want to examine briefly these Christian evaluations of the three themes identified above, and to pose some additional questions in relation to these evaluations.

## (a) Criminal justice and social justice

An honest and self-critical appraisal of major social issues is obvious in each of the contributions. Commissioner McNee acknowledges the pressures on the police with regard to corruption.[35] Mike Jenkins identifies many of the shortcomings of prisons.[36] Bob Holman gives a balanced and realistic appraisal of the limitations of his involvement on a council estate in the face of pervasive social problems and structures of disadvantage.[37] A similarly honest evaluation of the frequent callousness of the general public with regard to the criminal and to other social problems is evident in Chuck Colson's chapters.[38] Professor Anderson clearly outlines the unresolved dilemmas of the criminal courts in approaching sentencing, and the shortcomings of the adversary procedure in criminal trials.[39] This hallmark of honest appraisal seems to me to be a necessary *starting point* in Christian evaluation though, of course, it is not exclusively a Christian trait.

The awareness of failure and a preparedness to consider change are underpinned by a carefully considered stand on certain fundamental principles. Some of these will appear 'conservative' in a secular evaluation and others 'radical'. They include a Christian commitment to the need for law, and for just means to control man's selfishness and greed.[40] This is seen as a counterpart to the justice of God and is to be exercised in accordance with his will.[41] It is, however, balanced by a clear recognition of 'structural evils' which restrict and damage the lives of individuals and lead to a range of social problems for them.[42] The protection of the weak and the disadvantaged and an encouragement to care for others in our 'me – generation'[43] are consistently stressed, whether in relation to an offender or to those facing other sorts of disadvantage.[44] It is not always possible to identify 'the' Christian response, though as the contributors write about their work, there is a clear balance between their concern for individuals and their concern to ensure that justice is done in a wider context. Both concerns are the product of a Christian love for one's neighbour, of a belief in the value and dignity of the individual,[45] and of the calling to work for a more just social order.[46]

*(b) The responsibility of the individual – absolute or negligible?*
Chuck Colson concludes that the Judaeo-Christian view of sin (and of crime) is that the individual must ultimately be held responsible for his conscious decisions.[47] This assumption is central to a Christian evaluation of what criminal justice entails. After a careful review of the different philosophies of sentencing adopted by the courts, Professor Anderson expresses the Christian evaluation that the courts have a duty to lay down a penalty based on a 'tariff' system, so that like offences are in principle dealt with alike.[48] While he argues that this should be the fundamental approach, he also suggests that there is a place for explicit departure from the imposition of what is an appropriate penalty in particular circumstances. Inevitably, however, as Professor Anderson readily admits, this approach raises problems, specially in relation to the increasingly wide range of sentences which seek to have a rehabilitative effect on an individual (such as probation, community service orders, etc.). When the same sentence may have significantly different implications for different offenders, it is difficult to avoid appearing to treat like offences in an unlike manner.

Chuck Colson and Mike Jenkins deal with two alternative reactions of those in prison to their responsibility for what they have done: some appear to deny guilt,[49] while others become overburdened with a sense of low-esteem.[50] They argue as Christians that there is a need to recognize both one's own responsibility and the value of the individual in the sight of God.[51] This Christian position neither undermines the offender's integrity (by considering him to be of 'diminished' responsibility) nor leaves him without hope (in the face of his own weakness and failing). Christian conversion – with its emphasis on repentance, forgiveness and a new allegiance and empowering – reaches to the heart of these needs of every individual.[52] Both authors stress the importance of individual Christians serving as prison staff or as volunteers, who share their knowledge of Christ with offenders and seek to bring them into the caring community of local churches on their release from custody. This activity is part of the continuing work of God in 'proclaiming liberty to the captive' and making his Kingdom a reality.[53]

### (c) Controlling crime and dealing with offenders

Is it possible to form a Christian view on what measures should be adopted to control crime and deal with offenders? Judging from the wide range of positions taken by Christians on such contentious issues as the death penalty and corporal punishment, the achievement of a coherent Christian view may seem a pious dream. Professor Anderson deals with the principles underlying his own position as to the types of penalty which can be endorsed by Christians,[54] and he, Chuck Colson and Mike Jenkins all draw attention to the conscientious questions Christians must ask about the 'deformative' rather than 'reformative' aspects of prison experience.[55]

The emphasis of both Mike Jenkins and Chuck Colson on the integrity and the value of the offender as a person must lead to their rejection of more extreme ways to control the behaviour of offenders namely through surgery, drug control, etc. There is certainly, however, a need for further exploration of the relationship between learning as a positive part of a sentence (especially in prison)[56] and some of the more positive forms of behaviour therapy and social skills learning which are gaining ground in the work of prisons and day centres for offenders. Presumably such help ought to be available on a strictly voluntary basis as it would otherwise lead to major critical questions about the rights of any society to impose certain norms on any of its members.

Christians will inevitably hold divergent opinions as to the appropriateness both of police powers and of particular sentences on offenders. What is needed is clear and detailed argumentation of the principles at stake, probably more closely related to the dilemmas posed by real-life cases. (D. A. Thomas's book on the sentencing practice of the Court of Appeal is a particularly valuable source of information on how the principles are adapted to the complex reality of sentencing[57]). Perhaps the question of the principles involved in sentencing is most significantly raised in relation to the dangerous offender. With increasing concern to limit the amount of imprisonment, the problem of dangerousness has become of central importance, and Christians need to make a serious study of it. It has far-reaching implications for long sentences based on largely unpredictable risks of future repetition of particular crimes.[58] It also raises ethical issues about how we take account of the capacity for change that individuals may or may not have.

**Directions for change**
It is appropriate that the contributions to this book combine critical analysis with a variety of suggestions for change. In conclusion, I want to draw together some of these which the reader may pursue further if he so wishes. They can be loosely grouped under three general headings:

*(a) Suggestions for change in the structure and procedures of the criminal justice system*
These include:
> changing elements of criminal procedure[59]
> widening the range of sentences available to courts, including the use of restitution and community service[60]
> reducing the use of prisons and the length of prison sentences[61]
> developing the role of the local prison[62]

*(b) Suggestions for change in the wider social context*
These include:
> different ways of preventing crime, including 'target-hardening'[63]
> community social work and fostering good community relationships[64]
> redressing the balance between the wealthy and the disadvantaged[65]

*(c) Suggestions for Christian involvement*
These include:
> living in deprived areas[66] and being involved in their community life.
> making contact with offenders on a one-to-one basis and linking them into local churches[67]
> pursuing careers in the police service, the prison service, etc.[68]

These and other suggestions, which can be found throughout the chapters of this book, provide a full agenda for action for all those who are concerned to see justice in our democracy. None of the contributors glosses over the problems involved in change or in any of these forms of involvement, either for society as a whole or for individual Christians or local churches. Bob Holman points out the failures of the Christian community in relating to deprived areas, and modestly adds the limitations of his own involvement in community work on a council estate.[69] Chuck Colson provides an honest and self-critical evaluation of the many difficulties which may be encountered in the formation of one-to-one relationships in and outside prison.[70] Mike Jenkins sadly acknowledges the broken nature of the 'body of Christ' in the prison setting and the difficulty of transcending the in-built barriers between 'screw' and 'con'.[71] For all the constraints and shortcomings of the criminal justice system in which they are working, each author proceeds on the basis of hope and commitment, which derive from obedience to the commands of Christ and are worked out in a response of care and concern for others. Their experience of the love of Christ in their own lives leads them to make the same experience a reality for those with whom they are involved.

# Notes and References

1 Pages 16–18.
2 Pages 26–28.
3 Chapter III, especially pages 72–74 (historical perspective) and pages 76–80 (discussion of the balance between the protection of the community by the police and the freedoms of the individual).
4 Pages 81–85.
5 Pages 118–120.
6 Pages 98–101.
7 Pages 134–135.
8 Pages 19–34 and 96–101.
9 Two recent reviews of explanations of crime and responses to it in Britain since the Second World War are a series of articles by Stanley Cohen in *New Society* (March 1, 15, 29, 1979) and David Downes' review, 'Promise and performance in British criminology', *British Journal of Sociology*, 29, 4, December 1978, pp. 483–502.
10 The conflict arising from the creation of the Metropolitan Police is alluded to in Chapter III, page 72. See also Michael Ignatieff, 'Police and people: the birth of Mr. Peel's "blue locusts"', *New Society*, 30.8.79, pp. 443–445.
11 See, for example, President Carter's comments quoted on pages 21–22.
12 Samenow and Yochelson's findings are discussed on pages 31–34. See also Enrico Ferri's observation quoted on page 22. Patricia Morgan's book, *Delinquent Fantasies* (Temple Smith, 1978), is a recent British critique of 'liberal' assumptions about the causes of delinquency.
13 Page 37.
14 Pages 37–38.
15 Pages 101–102.
16 These are highlighted by the Wilson and Herbert study, *Parents and Children in the Inner City* (1978), discussed on pages 99–101 and exemplified by the family facing eviction described on pages 118–119.
17 The case of 'Nick' cited by Chuck Colson (pages 24–25) is a notable example.
18 Bob Holman's community social work project in Bath described in Chapter IV is an example of an approach focussed on delinquency in a wider social context.
19 This divergence is discussed on pages 105–106. A fuller examination of

the issues involved may be found in Marcel Berlins and Geoffrey Wansell, *Caught in the Act* (Penguin, Harmondsworth, 1974).

20 These different approaches to sentencing highlighted by Wootton and Thomas are discussed on pages 62–64. Proposals for the 'decriminalization' of certain offences and diversion of offenders before sentence are considered on pages 137 and 162.

21 Pages 76–81. Michael Zander has reviewed research evidence relating to some aspects of police work in his article 'What is the evidence on law and order?', *New Society*, 13.12.79, pp. 591–594.

22 Chapter V, especially pages 135–136 and 140–141.

23 Pages 136–140 and 162–165. An official review of trends in British criminal justice policy in the decade 1966–1976 can be found in *A Review of Criminal Justice Policy, 1976* (HMSO, 1977).

24 Pages 55–58 and 161.

25 Pages 14 and 41.

26 Pages 29–31, 124–125 and 152–162. See also Bob Holman's discussion of reconviction statistics for penal institutions for young offenders, pages 103–104. Two noteworthy studies of the effectiveness of such institutions in Britain are Richard Ericson's study of a detention centre, *Young Offenders and Their Social Work* (Saxon House, 1975), and the comprehensive research on Dover Borstal, *Criminals Coming of Age* (A. E. Bottoms and F. H. McClintock, Heinemann, 1973).

27 Pages 29–31, 140 and 155–160.

28 Pages 136–144 and 162–165.

29 Pages 107–120.

30 See pages 74–75, 95 and 132–134. In addition to discussions of trends in offences and in sentencing contained in the annual volumes of *Criminal Statistics for England and Wales* (HMSO), the Home Office has recently published a comprehensive review, *Statistics of the Criminal Justice System, England and Wales, 1968–1978* (HMSO, 1979).

31 See pages 137–140 and 173–174.

32 Pages 16, 53, 87 and 128.

33 Pages 54–55, 77, 88 and 128–129.

34 Pages 113–114, 129–132 and 174–178.

35 Pages 85–86.

36 Pages 140–142 and 143.

37 Pages 118–120.

38 Pages 22–23 and 173.

39 Pages 59–60 and 61–64.

40 Pages 34–36, 53–54 and 77.

41 Pages 51–53, 87 and 127–129.

42 'Structural evils' are discussed in general terms on pages 37–38; examples of their impact on poor families and on sections of the prison population are cited on pages 99–102 and 134–135 respectively. Among many individual examples of their outworking are the cases of Becky (page 17), Ann (pages 84–85) and the family described on pages 118–119.

43 Pages 26–27.

44 Mike Jenkins emphasizes the role of positive relationships in prison (pages 129–130 and 142); Bob Holman outlines the objectives of his community social work project (pages 107–108); Chuck Colson discusses the work of the Prison Fellowship (pages 174–176).

45 Pages 113–114, 129–130, 177 and 178.

46 Pages 37–38, 88, 104–105 and 107, 127–129.

47 Pages 34–36. A similar conclusion is reached by Sir Norman Anderson (pages 51–53), Sir David McNee (page 82) and Bob Holman (page 98).

48 Page 64.

49 Pages 140 and 169.

50 Pages 166–168. See also page 114.

51 Pages 35–36, 38 and 166–168. This Christian approach was persuasively argued for by C. S. Lewis in his essay, 'The humanitarian theory of punishment' in *Undeceptions* (Geoffrey Bles, 1971).

52 Pages 36–40, 144 and 168–172.

53 Pages 129–132 and 174–176. See also Bob Holman, pages 117–118.

54 Pages 54–58: cf. Islamic law and practice, pages 66–67. Oliver O'Donovan's booklet *Measure for Measure: Justice in Punishment and the Sentence of Death* (Grove Books, 1977) provides further material on a biblical approach to the theological and ethical issues involved in punishment.

55 Pages 49, 140 and 153–162.

56 Pages 130 and 142. Both Mike Jenkins (page 144) and Chuck Colson (pages 168–172) see Christian conversion as the most 'radical' form of 'learning'.

57 D. A. Thomas, *Principles of Sentencing* (2nd edition, Heinemann, 1979), discusssed on pages 63–64.

58 See page 49 (and footnote 9 on page 68) and pages 135–136.

59 Pages 59, 60, 76–80, 137 and 162.

60 Pages 138–139 and 163–165.

61 Pages 49, 137–140 and 162–165.

62 Pages 142–144 and 173.

63 Pages 106 and 137.

64 Pages 83–85 and 107–117.

65 Pages 17 and 104–105.

66 Page 107.

67 Pages 107, 130–131, 143 and 174–175.

68 Pages 106 and 129.

69 Pages 107 and 118–120.

70 Pages 175–178.

71 Pages 130–132.